THE SCHOOL

*Essays on Moral and Social Education in
the Scottish Secondary School*

by

JAMES K. SCOBBIE

*With best wishes
James K. Scobbie*

First published in Great Britain 1984.

ISBN 0 950986 70 4

Copyright © James K. Scobbie.

The publisher acknowledges the following publishers and authors or
their representatives for the use of copyright material:
Stopping by Woods on a Snowy Evening © Robert Frost;
    Jonathan Cape Ltd.
The Little Girls © Elizabeth Bowen; Jonathan Cape Ltd.
The Hollow Men © T. S. Eliot; Faber and Faber Ltd.
Quotation from *Collected Poems of W. B. Yeats* by permission of
    Michael B. Yeats and Macmillan London, Ltd.

Typeset by E.U.S.P.B.,
1 Buccleuch Place, Edinburgh EH8 9LW.

Printed and bound by
Billing and Son, Worcester.

Contents

Acknowledgements

I acknowledge with gratitude assistance I have received from various friends in the writing of *The School Experience*: my late brother, Harry, ex-rector of Bankhead Academy, Bucksburn, for his detailed and constructive criticism of the ideas and language in the first draft; Robert Innes, Director of Continuing Education in the University of Stirling, and Ian Collie, Director of Education for the Central Region, for reading the manuscript and making a valuable appraisal of its contents and style; Dr Graham Jones of the Department of Librarianship in the University of Strathclyde, and Ian Morris, formerly Principal Teacher of English in Airdrie Academy, for their useful criticism of several ideas expressed in the book, prompting me to reconsider their validity; Mrs Nancy Brown for tirelessly and cheerfully typing draft after draft of the manuscript, and my former pupil, Mrs Jean Stirling, for reading proofs with care and commitment.

I am especially grateful to my former Director of Education, Dr John S. McEwan, not only for his discriminating observations but for his persistent encouragement without which the book would probably never have found its way into print.

Introduction

It is time to examine some of the far-reaching changes at present being effected in our educational system and to consider their significance.

Curricular development is much in the air particularly in that area on which our national prosperity probably depends — the study of the computer sciences and the mastery of their skills. The brightest of our young minds must be orientated so that they move at ease in electronic labyrinths stretching to infinite horizons. We dare not fall behind other countries in training our children to use these new concepts and new techniques for transforming the processes of living into hitherto unimaginable shapes. We must keep abreast of and, if we can, outstrip our rivals. Assessment and reassessment of our progress will have to be continuous and thorough. If there ever was a possibility that examinations would diminish in importance, as some had hoped, such a notion would now carry no weight in a system which, as far as the more able pupils are concerned, has become indisputably vocational and competitive.

In Scotland a more liberal philosophy may underlie developments affecting all pupils, not just the more able. New courses and curricula have been devised to enable even the weakest pupils to work at levels commensurate with their ability in a wide variety of subjects and to acquire appropriate qualifications at the end of their fourth year in the secondary school. The new Standard Grade examinations may be taken at three different levels — Foundation, General and Credit. Less able pupils will no longer be abandoned to non-certificate courses as in the past. All this will, one hopes, bring about a revival of spirit in our school societies with everyone having something to work for within his or her capacity and being aware of some kind of progress. The new examinations are to be structured with a place for continuous assessment and internal and external moderation. The intention that some of the pressures should be removed from examinations is laudable. But one fact must not be overlooked — that we have opted for more examinations, not fewer, quite a reverse situation from that which the more idealistic educationalists of twenty years ago would have envisaged.

Emphasis on the importance of examinations will be heightened by the introduction of 'parental choice' with respect to the promotion of children from primary to secondary schools. To assist parents in making a choice of school the statistics of examination passes and failures are to be made available for inspection. The motives of parents who have welcomed this change are far from public-spirited. They are not interested in the overall quality of our educational system. Indeed parity of examination performance among all the schools in their district is the last thing they would want. They want only two things: that some schools should be more efficient at preparing pupils for examinations than others and secondly, that they should obtain places in one of the more efficient schools for their own children. A result of this development will inevitably be that schools in the interest of their survival will have to concentrate on examination attainment frequently to the neglect of non-quantifiable objectives.

Is there a danger that obsession with examination results may cause us to lose sight of long-term objectives in education? In many subjects success in examinations is a short-term objective. With the exception of subjects that may be a preparation for subsequent studies at tertiary levels, most pupils forget almost all they have learned for examinations a few years after those examinations are over. A school should surely have something more to offer than packages of knowledge designed specifically for examination requirements but little else. Have we abandoned the idea once universally accepted that the purpose of education was to develop all the potentialities of our pupils, intellectual, aesthetic, physical, social and moral or, to put it another way, to produce complete persons? Is it still one of our aims to make good citizens? Are we really in earnest about social and moral education? If our pupils acquire dangerous, anti-social habits in our school playgrounds, are we to disclaim responsibility on the grounds that the school's primary role is to prepare pupils for examinations?

One sometimes hears the phrase, 'the hidden curriculum'. This would connote the formation of habits, attitudes and values many of which are not implicit in the material studied in the various classrooms. These things are not taught. They grow. They are experienced by the pupils if the climate of the school is favourable to their growth. And this means that the school would be a stable community with a vigorous lifestyle, a concern for ethical obligations and a tradition of dedicated service among the teachers. In such a school, too, the vision and leadership of the head would be of paramount importance.

The nature of that school experience and the means by which it may be created is the subject of this book.

Chapter 1

Education for Examinations

Children between the ages of twelve and sixteen attend secondary schools and adults, in the role of teachers, are in charge of them. For six hours each day, five days in the week, forty weeks in the year, these teachers have one duty — to create conditions under which their pupils will develop into people somewhat different from what they would have been if they had never attended school at all. All processes initiated, maintained and completed by the teachers are based on some conception of an 'end product' however vaguely defined. Assessment, therefore, of the success of any teacher or school or system will involve identifying the aim or aims of the teacher or the school or the system under review.

There will inevitably be wide differences in the aims which various teachers will claim to have and most teachers would assert that they were trying to achieve a variety of aims in disparate fields — vocational, intellectual, cultural, aesthetic, moral, social and so on. But if one examines realistically the areas on which most secondary teachers concentrate, often to the exclusion of some other obligations, it will be found that the overriding concern is to achieve the maximum success for their pupils in the national external examinations. The syllabuses on which they work with most of the classes from first year onwards are structured with that end in view.

Coaching, training, teaching, cramming, single-minded concentration on passing examinations — it is a simple conception but one that continues to raise certain pertinent questions. One might well ask, for instance, whether teaching with examination success as one's sole aim is the best kind of teaching.

One must admit that it often achieves its purpose. Efficiency in any walk of life is not to be despised, and teaching specifically for exams certainly involves one kind of efficiency. Teachers who are concentrating on the preparation of their pupils for external examinations generally teach their subject more comprehensively, methodically, purposefully, consistently, assiduously and energetically than would be the case were there no exams: methodically, because an examination syllabus is generally set forth in a logical sequence, each stage leading on naturally to the next; purposefully, because awareness of the form in which the pupils will be tested will furnish a design for every classroom lesson; consistently, for the teacher must ensure that his pupils are equally conversant with every section of the syllabus; assiduously, because there never seems to be enough time to cover all the prescribed work, and so the teacher dare not relax his efforts at any time during the session; and energetically, because his object will be to take the maximum number of his pupils through the exam and he will try to compensate for lack of effort on the part of his weaker pupils by increasing his own.

It could be argued, too, in favour of the examination system that, apart from the success attained in terms of exam passes, the pupils learn that nothing of value can be obtained without hard work and some sacrifice of day-to-day pleasures. They learn the discipline that consists of concentration on lessons by day and long hours of evening study.

But when examination success provides the main motivation, it often replaces more desirable attitudes, a love of learning for its own sake or a wish to master a subject to a depth far beyond the demands of the syllabus. Few pupils experience such promptings nowadays. Their concern is passing the exam; they concentrate on the previous papers and the types of question likely to be asked. The idea that they might obtain enjoyment from studying a subject is a notion that rarely crosses their minds. All kinds of shortcuts to exam success and means of bypassing the more difficult parts of the syllabus with impunity are examined. Cramming books are bestsellers nowadays. Important sections of the syllabus are neglected because of shrewd calculations that one can avoid them by concentration on easier options. Few pupils reveal enthusiasm for their subjects by, for instance, purchasing books or equipment to facilitate private study and research. Love of learning is the rarest of phenomena — it does not rate a mention.

The main justification for the examination system is that external exams are an indispensable stage in vocational education. School courses leading to passes in the Highers in Physics, Chemistry, Biology and Mathematics constitute a necessary foundation for post-school education leading to careers in industry, science, technology, engineering and medicine. Moreover, the evidence provided by examination results is all important in the selection process for entrance to university and other centres of tertiary education. One should remember, however, that a considerable number of pupils who leave school with qualifications that would seem to be related to their future careers find themselves in positions where the knowledge acquired is not used. The truth is that no school can possibly offer the innumerable courses that would be relevant to the new modes of employment which, to keep pace with the bewildering advances in science and technology, proliferate with terrifying instancy.

In addition to the considerable numbers who pass the external exams but never thereafter use the knowledge or the skill they have acquired in their course, substantial numbers embark on courses leading to O-Grade or Highers and never attempt the exams at all. Somewhere along the line they voluntarily abandon the course or are removed from it in a state of ignorance and confusion. The many hours of teaching them subjects in a form geared to presentation for the external exam have been largely a waste of time. Mathematics, Physics, Chemistry, Biology, are ultimately abandoned by the majority and quickly forgotten.

It is difficult to avoid this verdict on the examination system, that in order to produce a comparatively small number of students who will build directly on the knowledge and skill acquired at school as the foundation for their future careers, hundreds of thousands of teaching hours are being devoted to teaching children subjects which they will never use again at any time in their lives.

An exception to this generalisation must be made in the case of the practical subjects. A practical skill, even if not used in one's career, is never wholly lost. Skill always seems to be an asset, likely to emerge as a hobby in later life or to be used in do-it-yourself activities.

Let us turn to what might be described as the non-vocational subjects, those not necessarily leading to a career but valued as part of the pupil's general education: aesthetic subjects, the social sciences, foreign languages, subjects presented as being enlightening or culturally enriching.

Teachers of the aesthetic subjects, art, poetry, music, will argue that in preparing their pupils for examinations they will be developing powers of aesthetic appreciation which will accompany them into adult life as a spiritual enrichment. Teachers of the social sciences, history, geography, modern studies, economics, will claim that their specialist subjects, thoroughly mastered, will lead their pupils to an understanding of the world they live in and of how things come to be as they are; to insights into the complexities of economics and the issues that divide the political parties; and to a comprehension of the environmental factors that mould our ways of life. Sustained throughout their teaching career by devotion to the classroom situation and by belief in the importance of their subject, they visualise their successful examination candidates as adults who will live a rich, full life, maintaining the most civilised traditions of our society and casting their votes in elections with understanding and discrimination. The justification for what goes on in these classes would not be their applicability to careers but that they form a preparation for life. It seems obvious, therefore, that the most valid assessment of the success achieved in the school classes in these subjects should be made not by the external examination but by investigation of their lasting effects on pupils after leaving school. The question we have to answer is how the lives of average adults have been affected by what they learned in these 'general education' subjects, the aesthetic subjects, the social sciences, the languages, native and foreign, and so on.

Let us go out then, you and I, as Eliot would say, into the world and have a long hard look at our contemporaries, the 'men that were boys when I was a boy'. Let us run the rule over our associates, and ask them what they have retained from the subjects in which they passed Highers and O-grades long ago.

We shall first of all note that very few of them ever read a book of any quality, and many of them never read a book at all, do not even possess one. I am not referring to the denizens of the subcultures, the bingo, betting, hard-drinking fraternities. I am referring to every level of the social spectrum. Go into the villas of your opulent fellow-citizens, people with private yachts, caravans, houses worth fifty thousand, private swimming pools, everything it would seem that money could buy or avidity might want to possess, and you will rarely find a library. This of itself is not a proof of lack of culture, for, theoretically at any rate, some of the bookless ones may appreciate good music transmitted by the media, or may spend their Saturday afternoons in art galleries, or may follow intellectual discussions on the television. Still, if you consider that most of the material covered in school syllabuses was transmitted by the printed word, it certainly looks as if markedly few of the standard school subjects have stimulated enough interest to survive as serious adult interests.

Inferences may also be made from the newspapers that are most frequently and most widely favoured. In spite of the hopes of proponents of modern educational methods that these will encourage pupils to think for themselves, or to scrutinise all relevant facts before reaching a conclusion, most people seem to prefer the tabloid press to the quality journals and to accept, without reservations, the sensational slant on events provided by the banner headlines.

Again, in the matter of pure knowledge the memories of our fellow-citizens seem to be lamentably deficient. If you are a specialist teacher, test your former pupils in their knowledge of your own subject, should an opportunity present itself. You will find that, in most cases, the only item within recall will be some throw-away line, some trivial detail, which you may have mentioned but had no intention of stressing. Perhaps most significant and well worth meditating upon will be your discovery that the only scrap of knowledge which survives is associated in the former pupil's mind with a humorous incident in the classroom, or with some manifestation of the teacher's eccentricity. (On a TV programme recently, some former pupils of an illustrious grammar school were asked by an interviewer what they remembered of the history taught in that school. The sole item that seemed to have survived was the observation, made by Voltaire, that the Holy Roman Empire was neither holy nor Roman nor an empire.)

Practically every person in Scotland, up to the age of sixty, has studied English poetry approximately once a week for three or four consecutive school years. Ask any of them to quote ten lines of verse or to name half a dozen poets and then ponder upon their response.

But you may say that such subjects are not related to modern life. Well, consider two subjects which could not be more closely related to our material existence in the modern world, economics and modern studies. Both these figure prominently in the curricula of most schools; but industrial disputes are debated daily over wide areas of our land, publicly and privately, with no more than the barest reference to the first principles of economics or the complexities of global finance.

There is no need to labour our inadequacy in foreign languages. It is well known both here and abroad.

When we discuss the weather or the climate of a holiday place overseas, how often do the elements of geographical knowledge appear in our conversation (wind direction, temperature, pressure, contours, isobars, and isotherms)? Yet that kind of material is covered in the geography classes of all our schools.

Observe our fellow-citizen on safari, travelling at home or abroad for a holiday. He has certainly studied history for several years at school. Yet he views, with uncomprehending eyes, castles and cathedrals and walled medieval cities, pyramids and ancient monuments and standing stones, without being able to make a single relevant informed comment on what he sees.

From all the situations which I have instanced, one might conclude that the average product of our secondary schools has remained ignorant in spite of all the earnest teachers and comprehensive syllabuses, or he has not succeeded in retaining what he has learned, or has developed so little interest in these subjects that he has not troubled to keep himself abreast of them, or to refresh his knowledge from time to time.

All this is not intended to be an overall condemnation of the contents of modern subject syllabuses or of the methods in vogue at the moment. Probably it has always been the case that most school learning was forgotten shortly after examinations were over. Psychologists who study memory now recognise various depth of memory, to which the varying degrees of retention correspond. They speak of long-term memory and short-term memory. Students may have evolved a type of memory which operates up to the time of the examination and thereafter quickly clears the storehouse to make room for more useful material.

And, of course, material efficiently taught and seriously studied often remains in the hinterland of the memory, even although it appears to have been forgotten. If the study of the subject is resumed, even late in life, most of it will be recovered with less effort than when it was originally learned.

Nor must we forget that because of the speed of communication, which is a feature of modern living, and of the dominance of the media in our lives, our minds are being subjected to a flow of swiftly moving impressions, each being immediately replaced by a fresh one, to form a new kaleidoscopic pattern. Unpredicted flotsam and jetsam jostle for places in our stream of consciousness and monopolise our attention for a moment before being swept away by things apparently more significant because they belong to the latest moment. The thing in vogue, the thing that affects our personal interests, today's sensation, alone carries weight. Knowledge learned long ago at school does not stand a chance.

But when all this has been said, a suspicion remains that many people, supposedly educated, are more ignorant than they ought to be and that most knowledge acquired at school either evaporates or retreats into our mental hinterlands with indecent haste. Perhaps the trouble is that we have come to have little use for knowledge apart from its usefulness for passing examinations. Or perhaps we have lost all zest for intellectual pursuits, all love of learning for its own sake. Anyhow between school and after-school there are few bridges. And this no one seems to notice or regret.

But even if we have doubts about the permanent value of what is taught or learned in the examination-directed curriculum, most adults would be quite certain that their education was important, that they had experienced a complex of ideas, attitudes and values (apart from knowledge and skills) which had some influence on their development into the kind of persons they ultimately became. What this experience is, what it might be, what it should be is the subject of this book. Most of this experience is extra-curricular. But it would be quite misleading to make a positive distinction between it and the processes that operate in the classroom, for every classroom has its own values which colour the teaching of the subject and which will survive as part of the school experience, even if most of the knowledge and the skills are forgotten.

Chapter 2

Remembered Experience

The educative process is much more than the sum total of the syllabuses that are studied in various classrooms, much more than being steered to various levels of success in national certificate exams. There are innumerable factors in the life of any school that have an influence, good or bad, on the development of the pupils. Combine them all, as far as they affect an individual pupil, and we have a process that we may call *the school experience*.

Every teacher, knowingly or unknowingly, intentionally or unintentionally, contributes to the formation of the school experience, not only by his approach to his subject in class and by his role in the extra-curricular life of the school, but also by the example he sets in habits, attitudes, moral behaviour and by the values which give meaning to what he says and does in the school. The teacher who imagines that his role is nothing more than organising the study of his subject, putting material in the way of his students, operating mechanical aids, giving out worksheets and correcting the pupils' scripts — such a teacher cannot have considered that he is, in fact, a performer before an observant, receptive and critical audience. To some of his pupils he may be a model of excellence, to others, an object of derision, but to none is he an anonymous entity. Has he thought that, daily, he is the subject of conversation — that his mannerisms are mimicked, his sayings quoted, his eccentricities described, his opinions analysed, his character assessed not only in the playground and common room but in the homes of many of his pupils? The things he says and does may be the subject of conversations twenty and thirty and forty years on — his humorous remarks, his outbursts of temper, his kindly and his sarcastic sayings, his hurtful reproofs and his good counsel, his foibles and his prejudices. He will remain in the memories of many of his pupils long after all that he taught has been forgotten. In their memories, aye, in their dreams and mayhap, in their nightmares.

The elements that combine to form the school experience of any individual are multitudinous, multifarious, multiplex; apart from curricular studies they include not only conditions that may affect him as an individual such as the atmosphere which he feels in the various classrooms he attends, but also the impression he shares with his fellows, the awareness of belonging to a community, the spiritual climate of the school.

There is nothing new about this. When parents, concerned about the future of their children, talk about 'good' and 'bad' schools, it is the quality of the rest of the school experience their children might have that they are often thinking about rather than academic competence. It is surprising, therefore, that head teachers so seldom give top priority to their role as deliberate creators of the total school experience of the children.

If classroom subjects are held to be a preparation for the world of commerce and industry, the rest of the school experience is for many 'the stuff that dreams are made on'. It is that part of the school experience rather than the curriculum that abides in the memory and enriches the lifelong consciousness of pupils who have been graciously educated. It is the climate of the place which makes a lasting impact on minds at their most sensitive stage.

Of course the extent to which pupils may be affected by school experiences will vary among individuals, for each individual at school has a set of experiences that are personal and unique.

The number of variables in the life of a schoolboy is infinite. He may walk to school or travel in a crowded bus with fellow-pupils; there may be a common room for him to take his ease in at the interval or he may have to loiter in a windswept playground; there may be a dining-room which he may or may not use; he may enjoy school meals or dislike them; he may be lucky in his friends and classmates or he may find their company uncongenial; in some remote corner of the playground he may be bullied by protection gangs or he may escape such ordeals; he may find one or more of the school extra-curricular activities which interest and excite him or he may not; he may be lucky or unlucky in the teachers appointed to take his class — dull, interesting, enthusiastic, sympathetic, cold, boring, slack, severe or sarcastic; he may be fit to play and enjoy games or he may be denied the opportunity for various reasons; he may go on school journeys or expeditions or he may not have the chance; he may spend part of the day in a kind of coma, entranced by a dream of some 'lass unparalleled'.

But this book is about the communal experience of being on the roll of a school at any given time. The most significant aspect of such an approach is the place of personal relations — 'I and thou'. The school experience is made up of people. The school world is not a machine. In the words of Leibnitz, it is force, life, thought, desire.

If you ask adults about their memories of their schooldays, they will generally tell you about their teachers rather than the subjects: their personalities, their habitual sayings, their eccentricities, even their moral attitudes. As far as we can judge from things remembered, the school experience seems largely to consist of people and happenings associated with personalities and personal relationships. What people remember are episodes that have emerged from the school considered as a community.

The question which will never be answered is of course: is there anything of educational value (in the widest sense) in these memories? The memories I speak of are distinguished by their vividness. Some happenings are remembered because there was an element of drama — some delinquency, or punishment. Others because they had some element of the unusual. Then there were funny incidents and humorous remarks. But most of the memories are about happy experiences, red letter days, colourful events. Let us not forget that 'the days that make us happy, make us wise'.

I think that Wordsworth would have said that these vivid memories, being part of our permanent being, may have had a greater influence on our personal growth than much of the classroom teaching which occupied our minds up to the time of the exam and then vanished from our consciousness.

However that may be, these memories are often linked to emotions. The school experiences that acquire permanence in the adult mind are tinctured with colour and joy, with wonder and affection and surprise and the serenity of summer days in the sun. And sometimes too there will be pity and terror. 'Joy and woe,' says Blake, 'are woven fine, a clothing for the soul divine.' But whether school memories are of joy or woe, there will always be people, young and old, friends and foes, crowding the corridors. For school is not just a preparation for life — it is life itself, flesh and blood, mind and spirit.

Let us turn aside for a moment and look at a selection of typical recollections of school. You will notice that one does not just recall the happenings but the emotions that are associated with them. Event, setting, atmosphere reintegrate and we are back in a timeless country.

In these recollections, teachers now perhaps long dead keep their ancient places: the one whose moustache bristled and whose eyes glared through circular spectacles; the one who held the class spellbound with wartime reminiscences; the one whose courtesy was inexhaustible in his relations with his classes and who always greeted his pupils with a suave 'Good morning'. A pupil may have forgotten the pieces performed by the school choir but will remember the strict discipline imposed by the music mistress. ('Without discipline,' she used to say, 'no work of excellence can be achieved.') The things recalled are often those that extended the children's emotional range; the silence in the school assembly when the head spoke in moving terms of the passing of a well-liked teacher; the punishment that put an end to smoking in the boilerhouse; the ecstasy one felt on entering the brilliantly decorated hall at one's first school dance and the solemnly formal manners on which the old gym mistress insisted for such occasions; the head-master's apology to a pupil at morning assembly because he had wrongly doubted his word; the excursion to the Ballet Rambert which became an excursion to the world of dream; the English master evoking the pity and terror of Shakespeare's *Macbeth*; the school trip to Paris and the hysterical laughter of the party at the attempts of one of the group to order a glass of iron-bru in a French café; ghost stories during the first sleepless night at the school's outdoor centre; the terrifying moment as one faced the ten-foot leap over the horse at the school gym display; and the summoning of the last ounce of courage to make the leap; the day one admitted or was too scared to admit copying in a class exam; the visit, as part of social education to the geriatric hospital and the surge of compassion in the abode of the dying; the feeling of loving fellowship with comrades on darkening snow-clad moors during the adventure course; the sympathy of some teacher when one failed in the final exam; the English master who would not read out your essay to the class without your permission, lest he embarrassed you; the roses brought to you in hospital by your house mistress; the welcoming warmth in the school on a winter evening when you had returned to a meeting of a club or an opera rehearsal; the tense moment before the curtains opened on the play; the day you had to spend the whole interval picking up litter in the playground because you had been caught throwing down a paper bag; school excursions and holidays abroad and camps and operas and concerts and plays and general knowledge competitions and sponsored swims and garden fêtes to raise money for a school bus or for some compelling charity; the shame that was felt by the whole school when some offence committed by its pupils got widespread press publicity; the gym master who assiduously encouraged one 'never to surrender, never to give up easily'; the agony of the last mile in the cross-country race; the awesome silence at school assembly when the head prayed for the family of a dead fellow-pupil; the serenity of June days at cricket or sports or a class outing; the final ritualistic handshake from the head as, your schooldays completed, you passed through the hall doorway for the last time.

Can we draw a conclusion from such a list of random recollections? Clearly these are of a different character from the material transmitted from teacher to pupil in classrooms. Many of the former are unusual incidents whereas the classroom material is basically routine and to some extent repetitive. Unlike the forgotten classroom material, many of the remembered happenings have a dramatic or emotional component, not often encountered in the routines of teaching. But the main difference is just that what happens in the classroom, even with the free modern methods, is subconsciously identified by the pupils with pretence and simulation, a counterfeit of reality, whereas their memories are of the real life that goes on in the school outwith the classroom. One might almost say that to some children these events, recalled so vividly, are not peripheral fragments of the child's school experience but lie somewhere nearer the centre. If this is so, many heads and teachers are at fault in paying so much attention to the organisation of classroom studies, useful to so few, and in paying so little attention to the whole school experience, which may be significant to so many.

Why significant? Just because, as Keats said, one can be certain of nothing but 'the holiness of the heart's affection'. Among all the conflicting theories of education there must be a place for the education of the emotions. To extend the spectrum of emotional sensibility, to provide proper objects for the exercise of the feelings, to recognise the school experiences of excitement, joy, surprise, hope, compassion, curiosity, encounters with victory and disaster, the warmth of fellowship, awe in the presence of the numinous, wonder at the loveliness of nature and art, as components of a full, rich personality — all this should be as much the concern of the teacher as the routines of his subject syllabus.

Chapter 3

Social and Moral Education

Every school has a syllabus of social education but many of them are reluctant to concern themselves with the really dangerous and destructive elements in contemporary society. They avoid these unpleasant issues and concentrate on what might be described as education for leisure; hobbies, sport, aesthetic activities like painting, drama, folk-singing. The scheme followed makes pleasant reading: table-tennis, aero-modelling, trampolining, judo, bridge, badminton, chess, astronomy, photography, local history, guitar playing. These have the merit of contributing to the happiness of the school atmosphere. And in the context of leisure-time activities they offer a welcome alternative to the aimless street peregrinations which so often lead to vandalism and violence.

But we must not be content with introducing the pupils to enjoyable leisure activities. We must look steadily at the world in which we live, and define those areas of moral decay which we must try to prevent from affecting the atmosphere of our schools. We have the power to do much — if only we have the will.

Our survey of the problem may very well start at a very superficial level — our urban lifestyle which compares so unfavourably with those of many European countries. We observe generations of our fellow-citizens who have spent eleven years of their lives in a school, and during all these years have not learned to refrain from the following practices: depositing litter on the pavements of our streets; dumping refuse beside hedges on pleasant country roads; allowing their dogs to be at large in housing schemes; barging into shops without a word of thanks for someone who had courteously held the door open; chanting obscene songs on the terracing of football grounds; travelling by bus or train without paying one's fare; shouting in the streets at passers-by whom they do not even know; failing to offer one's seat to an old or infirm person on a bus. Most of the items I cite are just instances of bad manners but they are widespread and it seems absurd that, during all the years of schooling, people have not learned or been trained not to perpetrate such practices. There was a time, not so long ago, when children were trained to be mannerly by the devoted old headmistress in the village school. Are modern teachers quite incapable of doing the same?

A more serious blemish of our society is the liquor problem with the young. Most children have sampled intoxicating beverages, and some have become addicts, by the age of fifteen. Alcoholism, glue-sniffing, drug-taking are on the increase and our schoolchildren are deeply involved. Can the school disclaim responsibility for these tragic developments? A large proportion of serious crimes in the country (violent assault, murder, rape, dangerous driving) is caused by alcohol. Can schools remain silent on this question when television advertisements night after night are by their implications persuading our young men and women that the drinking habit is the badge of mature adulthood?

Whether the schools can or ought to concern themselves with another feature of our society — the obsession with sexuality in TV, films, advertisements, the theatre and ordinary conversation — is arguable, but it is, at least, certain that if frivolous attitudes to sex and widespread permissiveness are leading to more illegitimate births and broken marriages, the matter is very much the concern of educationists, for the broken homes produce broken-hearted children. Those who frame school policies about the relationships between boys and girls in school cannot afford to ignore the forces in the modern world that are making children sexually mature at an increasingly early age, but failing to make them morally or intellectually mature.

At a more philosophical level most of us would agree that naked materialism is the mainspring of most of our lives. Our motivation is activated by avarice. All kinds of evils follow: commercial dishonesty, the demanding of benefits that can be obtained only by damaging the interests of others and, saddest of all, our disavowal of any duties with respect to the poverty and suffering of the disadvantaged nations.

Apart from these specific social problems and evils, there has been a striking change in intellectual attitudes, in the way in which people express the ideas they may hold. Reasoned argument with an opponent has been replaced by passionate denunciation. The middle ground crumbles. People no longer say 'I think'; they say 'I feel'. Logical argument is drowned in the chanting of slogans. Intolerance and blind hatred have replaced civilised dialogue as the medium of political communication.

Is it too much to hope that schools can uphold intellectual standards as well as social ones, take a stand for balanced judgement, moderation, common sense? The field for the growth of these qualities is the classroom. And they will not flourish unless they are exemplified by the teacher himself. To exhibit these qualities as he teaches is one of the most significant contributions he can make to the pupils' school experience.

Many will object that the faults of society, with their unfathomable origins, can never be amended by a school's ethical code. But if not there, where? Children attend school six hours a day, five days a week, forty weeks a year, under the influence and authority of mature teachers. Every generation in our society has that experience. The school has means and opportunity and power to create standards of conduct and acceptable attitudes to social situations and problems. Schools have the resources. What they need is the will.

Social/moral education is often regarded as just one more subject in the curriculum to be allotted so many periods and to constitute a series of classroom lessons. But there is no certainty of the lessons taught in the classroom surviving in adult life and a deeper approach to the problem is called for. Let us think of the school as a garden rather than a factory. Results will come from fertile soil and favourable climate. Success with social and moral education and with the development of character will depend on the nature of the school considered as a community. The school community is an intricate complex of personalities acting and reacting in inter-relationships to produce an atmosphere which will largely determine the quality of life lived there. The creation of this climate lies largely within the power of the headmaster and his staff if they would only keep thinking about it. Their policies, their attitudes, their own behaviour will set the tone which will influence the manners and the moral attitudes of the pupils. For the tone of a school does not come by accident, and its creation demands as much attention as the conventional curriculum or as the manipulation of the machine that goes under the name of the management system.

What do we mean by social education, by moral education and by the development of character? These terms seem to correspond to different levels at which human life may be lived.

Social education is concerned with one's relations with other people in a group. It involves respect for other people's rights, their comfort, security, legitimate pleasures (i.e. pleasures that do not infringe the rights of others). It means that an individual must not seize for himself more than a fair share of any benefits that accrue in virtue of being members of the society. Vandalism, theft, violence, the careless disposal of litter, abusive, obscene language are all unsocial acts because they reduce unnecessarily the safety and comfort and composure to which fellow-members of society are entitled. Conceptions of good citizenship may go further. One may feel impelled to share and lighten the misfortunes of less fortunate members of the community and to turn natural feelings of compassion into positive acts of helpfulness.

Such is the type of material which would be appropriate in a school scheme of social education.

Moral education is surely something different and, in an age when determinism is the creed of most scientists, somewhat controversial. Moral education is based upon the belief that man has free will and the power to choose between different kinds of conduct and is properly held to be responsible for the choice he makes. Social education may well be a process of conditioning people to behave in a way acceptable to society; moral education would emphasise the options open to an individual with the corollary that it lies in his power to choose the good, the right option. A moral person, according to this way of thinking, will always have a sense of responsibility and a troubled conscience if he should make the weak, the selfish choice. He will keep any promise he makes; he will tell the truth; he will be just, even unselfish in his dealing with others; he will not exploit other people or their weaknesses for his own ends.

He will behave in these ways not because of the logic of some social contract, but because he believes that good is right and evil is wrong; that a choice between them is within his power; and that he accepts responsibility and will not, when he behaves wrongly, take refuge in excuses that would obscure the fact of his personal accountability.

To encourage such an attitude and to emphasise the beauty, the absolute rightness of virtuous conduct, would be moral education.

If such moral lessons are not explicitly taught in schools, the judgements made daily on the acts of individual pupils certainly suggest that this old-fashioned conception of good and evil still holds sway in the minds of teachers and parents. Telling lies, for instance, is still accounted a serious offence in most schools.

Of course this idea of personal responsibility and the absoluteness of virtue and vice, of good and evil, is a basic part of the Christian ethic and as such should take a prominent place in the lessons in religious instruction. The connection is not in dispute. It is possible or arguable that you can have morality without religion but what is certain is that you cannot have the Christian religion without morality.

How far these modes of moral behaviour are the subject of instruction will vary from school to school. But they have a deep reality in the heart of the school experience. When we think about or meet our former pupils in later days, we do not think of their attainments in the academic field so much as their personal moral qualities — whether they were honest or deceitful, reliable or untrustworthy, obliging or selfish. And when we come to write reports of them to employers or even to admission boards of universities, these vague abstract qualities, these moral strengths and weaknesses seem to have an important place. What one is is as important as what one knows.

It is possible that exception will be taken in some quarters to the language I am using to describe behaviour. Is it outdated, this talk of responsibility, conscience, virtue, duty? These terms may well be somewhat unfamiliar to the newly trained young teacher. In the educational literature he has studied at college, the treatment of behaviour appears to be the exclusive field of the sociologists and the psychologists.

The sociologists seem to be obsessed with the theory that our educational problems originate from the class structure of our society. They define the various classes in terms of occupations. Each class has its values which are, therefore, no more than social prejudices; they have no claim to absolute status. The values which most of our schools would wish to inculcate, honesty, loyalty, good manners, a sense of responsibility, are no more than scientific phenomena (sociology being assumed to be a science) and are dismissed, if they are mentioned at all, as 'middle-class morality'.

Many college of education psychologists would be similarly reluctant to accept the moral categories I am assuming in this book. Their attitude to the conception of 'evil' is evasive, non-committal. Their philosophy is generally deterministic — that man is the helpless creature of uncontrollable impulses and subconscious promptings. Such doctrines have an inhibiting influence on those who wish to promote moral education which depends on the assumption that the individual is responsible for his actions and should be answerable for these.

These sociological and psychological doctrines are even more unfavourable to our third conception in the area of social/moral education, character-building. Character is an unfashionable word. It is associated with the now maligned public school system, ridiculous ideas like 'the white man's burden', Kipling's ethic as detailed in *If*, 'the stiff upper lip', the charge of the Light Brigade and so on. But one must look squarely at the conception of character, for it implies the presence of positive personal qualities, the depth and splendour of which are unlikely to be appreciated by the educational sociologists, who think that education is a science to be described in clinical—and superficial—jargon.

Modern educationists may very well ignore 'character', but the schools cannot avoid recognising it when reports are to be completed for pupils' applications to universities and for posts in commerce.

What do we mean by character?

A person with character possesses some extra inner strength which he often shares with those who are associated with him in work and play. That is why the notion of character is often linked with qualities of leadership. He has reserves of moral strength which enable him to maintain a momentum when others hesitate and falter. He is recognised by his self-discipline, the restraint he exercises over his less creditable impulses. He controls his temper. He disdains the trivial and the shabby. He is more indifferent than others to his own material interests or even to his own reputation. If he refers to his own achievements, it is in modest terms. He accepts responsibility willingly and makes himself the vassal of his obligations. He is resolute and cheerful, more so as 'the sky grows darker yet and the sea rises higher'.

The admirable qualities I have described depend partly on heredity and home environment. It is not suggested that it is an obligation of schools to inculcate them in all their pupils. Yet schools recognise their existence and their value and have them in mind when school leaders and holders of offices etc. are chosen. Many schools deliberately set out to nurture the seeds of character when these are recognised. The dispatch of so many boys and girls to adventure schools, sea schools, skiing holidays, leadership courses, etc., is a recognition that it, the development of character, is in some ways a proper concern of the school.

The social evils of our time are there for all to see and schools must not close their eyes to them hoping that they will go away. Heads and teachers must think as persistently and purposefully about maintaining or improving behaviour standards in the schools as they do about the effectiveness of teaching in the conventional curricular subjects.

Those who wish to give some attention to this problem cannot ignore two aspects of the situation in school.

The first is that failure in the classroom seems related to deterioration in standards of conduct. Many of our pupils behave like good citizens up to about the age of fourteen, the time when they realise that they are trailing far behind in scholastic attainment, with the gap between them and the able pupils widening each month. This is the moment of truth, the depression felt in the classroom being deepened by the censure of disappointed parents. This is the time when large numbers of pupils, many of them of at least average ability, are classified as failures by a system which is concerned only with an obligation towards the élite. Without a word of comfort from their teachers (too busy with the prize list), they seek solace with fellow-pupils similarly placed and in their company develop an anti-school spirit which contrasts tragically with the joyous idealism which characterised their first entrance to the school two years previously.

One would hope that the present proposed changes in curriculum and assessment will brighten the horizons for the average pupil. For the present let us sustain them by our friendship, so that when they leave they will at least not feel impelled to shout disagreeable nicknames after us in the streets.

The second troublesome aspect is the moral debility of so many of our pupils. Problems of drink, gambling and sexuality arise from the lack of self-control, the ability to enjoy certain experiences in moderation. Another way of putting it is that there is a disturbing lack of self-discipline. Perhaps the school could take more to do with this aspect. It should be remembered that in olden days it was believed that self-discipline was linked with external discipline, a notion that many modern educationists would never accept. There are powerful influences in colleges and universities that belittle the conception of school discipline and believe that every problem of a behavioural nature can be solved simply by discussing it. These people have been more vocal and influential here than in other European countries and they have achieved disastrous results. It is a humiliating experience for British teachers abroad to hear foreign hoteliers speak with barely disguised contempt about the brash manners and insolent behaviour of British school parties.

Discipline! Was any great thing in history or in one's personal life achieved without it?

When we consider the long years children are under our tutelage in schools, we must, rightly, feel uneasy to see so many of our former pupils adopting lifestyles so depressingly different from the attitudes and standards of conduct that were accepted by them when they first came under our influence. Something went wrong somewhere. Could we not have done better?

Schools should be more positive about social training. Open-ended discussion groups are not enough. Our aims are vaguely formulated; our efforts random and unco-ordinated; our approach faint-hearted. Faced by the forces of permissiveness, the depraved tastes of the entertainment world, the jeering in the media at anyone who advocates virtue, we seem to have lost our nerve.

The challenge to the schools is formidable but we have to make a start somewhere and sometime. Consider the inculcation of good manners, an aim that no school would disassociate itself from. The school rules say 'Children are expected to be mannerly'. This will not take us very far. We should spell out rules of conduct for the children in the school and out.

Standards of civilised conduct should be insisted on and the pupils left in no doubt as to what is meant by good manners. The rules should include a code of good conduct, specifically referring to likely breaches of the code such as failure to respond politely to conventional greetings (e.g. 'Good morning'), to express thanks for services, to apologise when that is appropriate; obscene language; defacing of property with graffiti or similar acts of vandalism; improper disposal of litter; unsporting conduct, as players or spectators, at games. And, of course, there should be more positive items like welcoming strangers in the school, looking after new pupils, helping the disabled and so on.

In the way I have described good social conduct is something more than a recommendation, it is part of the discipline of the school. What we have to do is to train children to behave in a civilised way, and by training I mean something much more positive than teaching. Training implies insistence, pressure, drive, discipline, obligation, and sanctions against offenders. Schools should treat the training of good citizens as a high priority and tackle the task with determination.

So much for training in manners and citizenship. But there are more formidable challenges if we are concerned about the decadence of our society. If the schools are to contribute significantly to its recovery, it will be some kind of infusion of moral strength as well as training in conventional civility that will be required.

The last two or three decades have certainly not seen a strengthening of ethical standards in private and public life. Our motivation is mainly materialistic and the craving of most people for wealth and of many for prestige and power has often to be gratified at the expense of ethical principles. Dishonesty pervades the commercial world, big business and small trading, the advertising media, relations with tax and customs officials. We have the falsification of expense accounts at the higher level, fraudulent claims for public assistance at the lower. People nowadays are not expected to tell the truth, whether they are tradesmen who have not the slightest intention of honouring agreements, or world statesmen shamelessly lying in the face of overwhelming evidence of their shortcomings.

In the world of industry and politics, the terms duty, responsibility and obligation are nearly obsolete; the word 'rights', which no one can adequately define, has replaced them.

Drinking, gambling and sexuality are practised without moderation, uninhibited by the old-fashioned notion of self-respect. People are inclined to do what they feel like doing — and are never short of some psychological argument to justify it.

The social and moral education possible in a school would seem ludicrously feeble in the face of such widespread degeneracy. But one never knows. One has to start somewhere. And one way for the school to start is to look deliberately in the school community for pupils of character and contrive to place them in situations where they will set standards of behaviour and take the lead by their example in creating a school ethic. These should be well-known people, the more senior the better. They should be a kind of unofficial cadre, ever extending their influence, adding to their numbers. There should be weekend leadership courses to enable them to acquire attitudes to school behavioural problems and to sustain their morale. In their hearts the youth of today may have had enough of cynicism. Dedication, integrity, service, may be old-fashioned ideas but when presented without hypocrisy will be accepted as the basic foundations of the good life.

Whether these qualities can be instilled is arguable. Training in the armed forces is based on the assumption that character can, at least, be improved and a firm policy in a school, aimed at developing these qualities, might very well raise standards of conduct throughout the school community.

The picture of the responsibilities of a school towards its pupils, presented here, is unequivocal. One must reject the oft repeated statement that such-and-such is, or should be, the business of parents — is therefore not the concern of the school. The usual argument is that it is the business of the parents, and not the school, to train the children in good manners, truth-telling and so on, and this is perhaps how it was at one time. The conditions under which families grow up nowadays frequently do not allow of the co-operation of the parents in the educational process. Time was when the mother spent much time with her family, teaching them all kinds of traditional lore and precept, anything from nursery rhymes and proverbs to how to behave at parties. Broken homes, the frequency of employment of mothers, the new social customs which take the parents out to bingo or social clubs — all these have conspired to reduce the influence parents have on their family. And then there is the influence of notions of the generation gap and the exclusiveness of the teenage world, a theme unremittingly harped on by commercial interests, whose aim is to create a teenage market in clothes or music in which young people, better off financially than they ever were, can be exploited to the full.

We can no longer depend on parents. If we wish our children to grow up to be good citizens we must attend to it in our schools — or at least try.

But we need not think that we shall win general approval if we place honesty, the honouring of promises, the fulfilment of obligations, the respect for rights, the property and the person of other people, especially of those weaker than oneself, at the top of the list of priorities in the school's code of conduct. Some schools have taken an uncompromising stand on such issues and have, in the process, had to endure the ridicule of the 'progressives'.

Here is an extract from a letter in *The Sunday Times* of 4th August 1968:

> 'At a recent meeting of over four hundred former pupils of one of the most famous girls' public schools, the headmistress reported on a visit by three members of the Public Schools Commission. The criticisms of the school expressed during the discussion with them were so extraordinary, if not horrifying, that they are worth noting:
>
> Too much time was spent on inculcating ideas of service ('not necessary as there was a welfare state', as the commissioners put it).
>
> Too much time was spent in encouraging habits of courtesy and good manners.
>
> Too much attention was paid to the training in the achievement of 'high moral standards' (the reason given being 'that such training would make it difficult for the girls when they went out into the world and became involved in, say, industry').'
>
> Letter from Ian O. McCluckie, Hatfield, Herts.

The apostles of freedom in the contemporary educational scene maintain that schools have no right to instil behavioural standards — children must be left free to find their own values. This specious argument ignores the fact that in the world outside school, there are many individuals and groups who have no scruples about indoctrinating children, so that they can exploit them as, for example, the advertisers of teenage commodities or the purveyors of pop culture with their advanced views on sex and drugs and anarchy. Nor must we forget those who campaign to capture the minds of the young from political motives — adults who encourage children to form disruptive rebel groups in their schools, with the long-term aim of softening up the body politic in preparation for the great day of revolution. When all such groups agree to stop the indoctrination of young people, it will be time to question the presentation of moral and social values by the school.

The usual argument beloved of the sociologists is that the values I recommend are middle class, a simplistic generalisation that will not bear examination. Most of them are in keeping with the teachings of Christianity. (Incidentally, they would have been warmly approved by the founders of the Labour Party, many of whom were Methodist local preachers.) When the sociologists devalue these principles by their clinical analysis, I ask them, 'With what values would you replace them?'. Telling the truth, doing your duty, respecting your fellows, helping the weak, are not the marks of social class differentials. To my way of thinking they are absolutes. These qualities are to be found right across the social spectrum and the implication that their presence is no more than a badge of material and professional status is an insult to good-living working-class families who observe these values but borrow them from no one.

An ethical code, in school or elsewhere, must be presented within a frame of reference. The values I am recommending have been articulated, cogently and memorably, in the New Testament. If associated with morning assemblies and religious instruction lessons, they may acquire a relationship with school traditions and routines and even become a positive force in the daily school experience of the pupils.

Chapter 4

Offering Alternatives, Social and Moral

There is no escaping our obligation to try to create acceptable social behaviour in the schools. Where fifteen hundred young people are rubbing shoulders with one another for six hours each day the quality of inter-personal relations is all important. School is not merely a preparation of life; it is life itself. Our children must be safe, safe from violence, from being exploited by older pupils, safe from moral corruption. They should be as happy as we can make them. We have the power to do so and the duty, for some will die young and we do not know what fraction of each person's life is to be lived in the school. 'There with the rest are the lads that will never be old.' The school experience should be a model of how good and satisfying life might be.

As we consider the nature of the school experience, we must ask ourselves how far are we to accept in school the values of the society which the pupils will ultimately enter. How far are we, as teachers, justified in taking it upon ourselves to offer to the young an alternative set of values, which will conflict with those which the pupils know to be the standards of the world which they will enter when they have left school.

Many of that world's undesirable habits and attitudes are accepted by children without question through their observation of the behaviour of adults. They will not know any better. It would, however, be profitless and unrealistic to concern ourselves in school with the follies and vices of the adult world; we are likely to be more successful if we concentrate on the modes of anti-social conduct that prevail in the lives of our pupils. We must concentrate not on vague, hypothetical situations in the far future but rather on the selfish, ill-mannered and occasionally vicious conduct instances of which we encounter day by day in the schools.

Here are some attitudes and habits that I believe to be widespread.

Many pupils have no compunction about interfering unjustifiably with others, whether by bullying or by ridiculing their appearance, or by jeering at them when they are in embarrassing situations or when they adopt a line of conduct different from the norm. Exploitation through protection rackets and the pressurising of earnest scholars not to co-operate with the classroom teachers are not uncommon.

Many pupils lie spontaneously and shamelessly. No moral turpitude is experienced on such occasions. Integrity is not recognised as a meaningful status.

An inclination to casualness, regarding personal appearance, punctuality, civilised manners is prevalent. 'Self-respect' is an obsolete notion. It is doubtful if the conception is understood by many of our pupils.

Cheating, whether in examinations or by avoidance of paying one's fare on a bus journey, is the normal practice. The idea that such conduct is detrimental to the interests of others would carry no weight.

Respect for one's physical environment (in this case, the school's) seems with many pupils to be non-existent. Litter, graffiti, vandalism and such evidence of juvenile insensitiveness are encountered everywhere and seem to be out of control.

Traditional sportsmanship is outmoded. One plays to win and only to win. Beaten opponents are jeered at. Gamesmanship is acceptable; rules are interpreted by letter and not in the spirit. Failure to control one's feelings on the sportsfield when things go wrong (and when they go right) is now the norm. In general the brash attitude is the desirable one.

Obligations freely accepted are not honoured. Children join organisations and immediately leave them. They promise to attend a practice or a meeting and then ignore the engagement because something more attractive has turned up. This attitude is widespread. 'Letting someone down' brings no shame.

Such attitudes are prevalent in most school societies. The school must offer alternatives to these. These alternatives will not necessarily be expounded in the classroom but will be presented mainly as part of the school's ethical code. More important will be the exhibiting of them in real situations. They should be exemplified in the manners, behaviour and attitudes of the teachers. The teachers form a vital component of the school experience.

But one must beware of relying exclusively on a school ethical code consisting of prohibitions, creating a puritanical, scholastic Geneva, with the headmaster playing John Calvin.

The school lifestyle, the school experience, should be remembered for its colour, its vitality, its joy, its humour, its living traditions, its positive activities rather than its decalogue of prohibitions.

The school has to compete vigorously against less altruistic agencies in the world outside for the interest, the support, the loyalty, the involvement of the children concerned.

It must be happy and meaningful and appealing to young minds. It must offer the boys and girls a range of varied, satisfying, profound and memorable experiences, stimulating and opening out before them vistas of exciting and satisfying ways of living.

As a community it must be a reservoir of moral assets. It must be an image of the good society, characterised by concord and by tolerance of those who differ from us in race, culture and social level. The divisions that separate the able and the less able into mutually exclusive worlds will be replaced by a feeling of common involvement in a community greater than the individuals that compose it, a great loyalty, a shared affection for their school as their second home, an acceptance of one another.

If one takes the view that the general success of a school depends in a large measure on its qualities considered as a society, then it must be examined very closely with that in mind. One must study its atmosphere, the particular quality that one might identify in the lifestyle of the school, and this would be an amalgam of many different constituents. It would be a compound of the thoughts, the attitudes, the emotions, the aspirations, the hopes and fears, the manners and behaviour patterns, the habits of speech and costume of all people in the school, headmaster and staff and pupils and administration staff and auxiliaries, balancing the constant, prevalent, habitual or traditional elements, which might be called the groundwork or the soil, against the transitory currents of fashion or trends, so that each day would be subtly different from, but in some measure similar to, every other day. To identify unerringly the essence of a school society with a view to improving it would involve all the faculties and powers of the most sensitive of headmasters. But if the reality of a school depends on its atmosphere or climate of thought and behaviour, then it is all important that the authorities, the decision-makers, the originators of modes and of policies, should be right close up against the minds of the children, looking straight into these minds, observing and evaluating them both as individual entities and in the mass.

Chapter 5

The Climate of the School Community

Individual regeneration usually comes from communal strength. Habits are acquired by imitating those with whom one lives and works. Esprit de corps is not a meaningless cliché, an outworn joke — it is a fact of life. Strength and inspiration and standards of conduct are acquired more easily when they are part of the traditions of the regiment with which we march. In Cromwell's words, we 'know what we fight for and love what we know'.

Our concern must be, morning, noon and night, the state of the nation, the climate of the school community. Head and teacher must think about this daily, with the concentration of the priest studying his breviary.

Those who specialise in management may well think that the elements that go to make up the school experience are all taken care of in their system. I have seen brochures of fifty pages explaining how every branch of curricular and extra-curricular activity fits into the master plan. But I have also seen a steady stream of amendments to that master plan, following in bewildering accumulation. For a school community is a living organism, continually changing its being, and therefore demanding continuous observation. Its identity is in a state of development; its history unfolding day by day. Seemingly trivial and unpredicted acts, even words, of teachers or pupils may work a subtle change in the atmosphere on one classroom and even in the climate of the school. The source of nuclear reaction is minute. A single event in the school may invigorate the whole body politic; a reckless act may inaugurate an era of disruption. The barometer must be under constant inspection. The difficulty is that many heads assume that the system will take care of everything; they seemingly are unacquainted with the unpredictability of human affairs; existence is a succession of newly born episodes.

The quality of the total school experience should be the main concern of those who are in positions of responsibility and should be an element in the thinking of all teachers. Each one should keep asking questions about the atmosphere of the school, the general behaviour of the pupils, the standards that are implied in the school rules, the validity of the traditions, the respect which the school evokes from the pupils, their reactions of love and hate, of admiration and rejection. Changes in the atmosphere must not pass unnoticed. These may carry promise of a happy exciting development; they may conceal the seeds of danger.

The flow of school happenings, apart from their impact on individuals, evokes changes in the communal mood — bad weather, exam depression, holiday anticipation, a school show, a victory or defeat in some important match — such things bring joy or gloom. It is the business of those who govern to notice such changes in atmosphere, and when they see danger in their prevalence, to moderate them by judicious admonition.

Nor must the mood of the teacher in the classroom be left out of account. A teacher whose emotional instability is such that the children lined up in the corridor ask the emerging class, 'What mood is he in?" is making a shameful contribution to the school experience.

Let us never forget then that the life of a school community is an on-going thing — not a routine. At no point can it be left to take care of itself.

Even when the curriculum has been reformed in such a way that every pupil is studying his or her course subjects at a level where he or she is progressing, not regressing, even when there has been evolved a system of management by which every duty has been delegated, every role defined according to the current doctrines of job specification, the nature of the total school experience must still be the main concern of the head and his staff. The Sleeping Clergyman in James Bridie's play of that name was thought to represent God who started it all and then went to sleep, letting things take their course. Some schools seem to be similarly managed.

It is strange that those responsible for planning school buildings continue to accept, as holy writ, the notion that there should be an administrative centre located as far away as possible from the class-rooms. This layout has only encouraged headmasters to remove themselves from their pupils and insulate themselves against any whispers from the real world of school — the thoughts, moods, aspirations, hopes, fears, imaginings and dreams which constitute the collective consciousness of the school and the identities of the individual pupils who form the community.

The good headmaster is a gardener, not a factory manager. The sensitive plants will fare better or worse according to the soil (to which the school traditions may be likened), the exposure to sun and wind and rain (the happenings and experiences of school), but also to the skill and the watchfulness of the gardener. You will find him in his garden, walking in the glimmer of morning, the glow of afternoon and, as the Book of Genesis says, in the cool of the evening.

Physical features are an important part of the pupil's experience, the external environment, the architecture and the furnishings and decor.

The influence of the scenic environment will, of course, vary according to the natures of the individual pupils — whether or not they are imaginative or aesthetically responsive to their physical surroundings. Decisions about the locations of schools are taken at administrative levels remote from those which are the concern of this book. It will be sufficient to express the hope that headmasters and teachers, fortunate enough to be appointed to schools loftily situated and commanding views of green champaigns, sunlit vales and distant blue hills, will not omit occasionally to direct the gaze of their pupils towards these serene uplands in the hope that some, some time, will experience a moment of vision.

Nor are interior architecture and decor our present concern. The era of strict functionalism is, happily, over and our new schools are planned with some concern for aesthetic amenities. Attractive recreational and circulatory areas abound. Good conversation is an aspect of civilised living and one would hope that the excellence of the decor would be reflected in the quality of the conversation of the pupils who frequent these places. The Stoics taught themselves philosophy in a sunlit porch in ancient Greece and in medieval monasteries the cloisters offered a retreat for the studious. Let us visualise our school corridors as places for civil communication, where something approaching serenity abides. Let us not forget that school is a place for being as well as for becoming. It should be a pleasance, if you will forgive the obsolete but lovely word.

But there is many a good school in a bad building and the reverse is also true. The essential school is not composed of bricks and mortar. When the King of Sparta was asked to show an ambassador the city walls, he pointed to thousands of young men drawn up in military formation, their sunburnt limbs radiating health, strength and fitness. 'These,' said the king, 'are the walls of Sparta.'

The climate of a school is continually changing, though this is often not perceptible at any given moment. Many apparently trivial events pass unnoticed at the time of their occurrence but later are seen to have been significant. Judgement and experience will be necessary to assess the potentiality of day-to-day events. One can make oneself a nuisance by over-reacting, a fool for not identifying seeds of danger. But what all must beware of is the illusion of permanence implicit in an over-refined system of management. The thing that happens is the thing one never thought of. Head teachers of the 'sixties will remember the day when the first pupil appeared with a shoulder-length hairstyle.

The atmosphere of a school is created by a multitude of factors, the decor of the building, the dress of the pupils, the style of government, the personalities of the staff, policies, decisions, fortuitous events. Probably the most important of the influences that mould the school's lifestyle will be the influence of headmasters and teachers, over a long period, provided changes in personnel are not frequent. Yet it is doubtful if one in ten teachers ever considers that he has a part to play in forming the school experience of his pupils. Too deeply engrossed in the business of teaching his specialist subject, too deeply enmeshed in the routines of school administration, he forgets that he is a person in the story of the pupil's school life.

I often think of that day in March 1765, when a young school-teacher, John Murdoch, eighteen years old, went by appointment to an inn in Ayr to be interviewed by the father of Robert Burns in connection with his application for the post of teacher in the little school being formed for a handful of children, including Robert, at Alloway. John Murdoch, perhaps not much caring whether he obtained the job or not, opened the door of the inn parlour — and walked into history.

Every teacher should, from time to time, ask himself what kind of appearance he is making in the drama of the life of the school, how far is he contributing to its health and happiness, how far has his influence reached beyond the confines of his classroom, and, most sobering thought, how will he be remembered.

The first and most important stage in the creation of a healthy school community is the widening of channels of communication between teachers and taught. We must achieve mutual understanding, mutual trust, mutual respect. The good school is one in which teachers and pupils feel themselves as joint partners in a great forward-going enterprise; where each has an individual contribution to make to the wellbeing and success of the community and understands the nature of the contributions of other people; where it is recognised that what the pupils and teachers have in common, in virtue of being members of that community, is more important than the differences in their roles. To obtain this unity, this growth of mutual understanding, all opportunities for meeting and talking should be welcomed.

The type of communication between teachers and pupils, likely to prove most profitable to both, is not by formal speeches at school councils, inhibited as these are by procedural restrictions, but by casual conversation arising in chance encounters. There will be no lack of such occasions if staff have not formed the habit of remaining in seclusion when they are off duty and are prepared to get out where the action is. Opportunities will occur in the playground at intervals, in the dining hall, on the touchlines at school games, on school journeys or outings, at social functions. The teacher will take the initiative but there will be no harm if the pupil does most of the talking, provided that he does not compromise the teacher's status by a disrespectful manner, or the teacher does not infringe the protocols of professional etiquette by allowing discussion about his colleagues.

Many benefits will accrue from such conversations.

The first is that the staff and the headmaster will learn what the pupils are thinking, and saying, to one another about the management of the school, the rules and the decisions. More important will be suggestions for improvement, and no teacher or head should be so authoritarian as not to listen to such contributions if seriously made, even by the youngest pupil.

The frequency of staff-pupil conversations will spread an atmosphere of concord through the school. The pupil will feel that he is not just a unit in a great impersonal wen; that he is considered of some importance to his teachers; that the school is a caring community. The mediocre scholars and the less attractive personality-wise, will be drawn into these conversations as well as the bright and charming ones. The hard lines of demarcation between the two school societies will be softened, and the privileges of citizenship will be seen to be available to all.

The tone of these conversations will be important. They may be the means of extending the civilising influence of the school. It will be incumbent on the staff to display good manners, to use courteous salutations, to imply, in what they say, their attachment to standards of honesty, fairness and consideration for others and to counter, even slightly, the coarse, aggressive manners which prevail in many of our playgrounds.

Many young teachers have an easy rapport with their pupils. The stuffy, dignified days are gone and most young teachers speaking, in a sense, the same language as their pupils, and being separated from them by only a few years, are in the best position to receive pupil opinions. It may be their role to act as intermediary between the children and the other members of the staff. With the right kind of headmaster the young teacher should be able to go and say freely, in words tactfully chosen, 'Some of the pupils are worried about the latest regulation'.

The good head would welcome this channel of communication for he, of all people in the school, must have his ear to the ground. He should be out and about at the changing of classrooms at the end of periods. He should stroll in the playground at many intervals. He should be a frequent attender at meetings of the Debating Society. He should be liable to put in an appearance anywhere where something is going on. He should stop pupils at random, in playground and corridor, and have a brief word, 'How are you settling down?' — 'Are you appearing in the first year concert?' — 'Did you enjoy your school lunch today?' — 'How are you finding third year maths?'. And pupils, in turn, should feel free to stop and talk to him.

In these rounds of casual conversations, the head, or someone else in an upper position, would be especially concerned with the weaker pupils. It is their trust, co-operation and respect that must be won and they must be persuaded, one way or another, that they are genuinely cared for in the community. The fact that someone of importance in the school stopped and spoke to them will certainly mean a great deal. And if, in addition to speaking to them, he is sharp enough to pick up their names, his hold over them, for the rest of their school careers, will be complete.

The emphasis should largely be on the establishing of ties of friendship rather than on making images of supreme, infallible authority. Respect for the head and his staff is a stabilising factor and entirely desirable. But this respect should be earned by the head's sincere and friendly concern for his pupils and their interests; it should not be assumed to be his right in virtue of his position. And one will not acquire respect by a continuous sojourn in the awe and mystery of the headmaster's study. A headmaster known to me visited a classroom where a second year class was located. He spoke briefly to the teacher and, with no more than a casual glance at the class, took his departure. 'Who,' said a curious pupil to the teacher, 'was that man?'

Teachers who mingle with the pupils in the manner I have suggested will gradually acquire an abundance of invaluable knowledge. To keep one's finger on the pulse, to make oneself acquainted with the attitudes of the pupils, both to traditional features and to innovations, should be the aim of every teacher who is serious about his obligations to the school at large, as distinct from his own department.

The people in the best position to know what the pupils are thinking are the teachers of Physical Education. The store of information the gymnastic instructors have built up about the characters, personalities and attitudes of children, as revealed in games in the gym or on the sportsfield, and the thoughts in their heads as expressed in the un-inhibited conversations in the changing rooms, form a bank of data which a wise headmaster will frequently find use for. For this and many other reasons, the role of the PE teachers in building the good school community is all important.

There is hardly any limit to the use which might be made of these casual teacher/pupil conversations. Often a piece of friendly counsel-ling, on the part of the teacher, would not come amiss — every teacher is a guidance teacher. And the school's ethical code, if it has one, should be sometimes quoted as the frame of reference in respect to judgement on some incident under discussion.

It may not occur to some teachers however, that this area of informal conversation is any of their business. Some of our most enthusiastic teachers are so engrossed in the work of their subject departments that they have little time to observe what is going on around them.

There are some who, if they saw smoking or heard obscenities in the school corridor, would think that the matter was someone else's concern.

Dylan Thomas's headmaster once encountered the poet (while a boy at secondary school) slipping out with his friends to play billiards in the afternoon. 'I hope you get caught," he remarked.

There are, of course, other ways of finding out what the populace are thinking. Articles in the school magazines or newspaper for instance. But one hesitates to recommend the use of the pupils' English composition as source material. These are personal documents often intended for the trusted ear of a well-loved English teacher.

'Tread softly, because you tread on my dreams.'

But there is no harm in asking the English Department to set essays on some school issues, telling the pupil at the same time that the head is anxious to learn their honest opinions. Most will respond trustfully if their relations with the headmaster are right.

This practice of social intercourse between staff and pupils develops a family spirit in the school. Through time it should result in growth of mutual understanding.

On the teacher's side a willingness to listen is all important. And, more positively, the teacher in these talks with pupils must display a standard of good manners, a civilised tone, with which the pupil's upbringing may not have accustomed him and which is markedly different from the raucous, barely intelligible bawling which passes for conversation between pupils, separated by some fifty yards, in the playground. If teachers say 'Good morning' or 'Good afternoon' to their pupils it is certain that they will reciprocate these salutations, and may even begin to use them in conversation with their fellow-pupils.

Teachers who are interested in social education (and all teachers should be), should realise that the first stage in the approach of the problem is for the teacher ·to see that his own behaviour is unexceptionable, for, if anything in this sphere is to be achieved, it will be by example rather than by lectures or classroom discussions. And the best way for a teacher to display good manners is in social relations and, particularly, in the informal teacher/pupil discussions that I have been describing. Teachers should never forget that they form probably the most important element in the pupils' school experience.

During the intermingling of staff and pupils on the campus, such as I recommend, incidents involving good and bad manners are bound to arise. Are manners important? It seems almost incredible that the inculcation of good manners, as an educational aim, would, in some quarters today, be regarded as a controversial issue. In the present state of our society, the rude, the abrasive, do not necessarily meet with condemnation. The voices of sociologists may even be heard defending such qualities as being acceptable departures from the much despised 'middle-class morality'.

To me, bad manners are acts of interference with the convenience, composure, comfort and ease of other people on occasions when they are doing one no harm.

They ruffle the surface of what should be a smooth stream of social intercourse. Bawling in playground or corridor creating disturbance to all within earshot; obtrusion without apology on conversations between teachers and other pupils; unmerciful jeering at fellow-pupils if the latter find themselves in embarrassing situations; failure to apologise when an apology is appropriate; failure to express thanks when a service has been given — these are daily occurrences in school.

To bemoan such behaviour in staffroom conversation leaves things as they are. The proper reaction, and it should never be neglected, is to condemn the action at the time it is observed, directly to the culprit, and in the hearing of as many pupils as may be in the vicinity.

As to life on the school campus one hardly need stress that the more frequently teachers circulate there, the easier it will be to curb the activities of anti-social elements in the school population. There have been bullies since schools first existed; protection racketeers and extortionists are perhaps more recent manifestations of the resource-fulness of the juvenile criminal mind. What is not always noticed is that the true schoolboy gang leaders wield more power over their class-mates than the teacher in the classroom does over these same boys and girls. Their activities include the pressurising of diligent pupils into abandoning their diligence and joining the cell of non-co-operators or issuing an edict to a whole class that they should cease to answer questions in certain classrooms. Addiction to smoking and to glue-sniffing often originates through playground contacts and the habit of expressing the simplest idea in strings of obscenity is readily acquired from the company of the more depraved citizens of the school. Complete elimination of such evils in large schools would be too much to hope for but efforts to prevent the corruption of the innocent should never be relaxed. It is a matter of grave concern that many pupils of average intelligence become progressively more confused in the classroom as they move upwards through the school; it is even more disquieting if some should grow progressively more vicious as well.

One obvious staff/pupil social area is the dining hall. Many schools have house dining rooms, where staff and pupils of the house are supposed to dine together. The obvious intention was that the corporate life of the house would benefit if pupils and teachers should share the same table. But we frequently see, in such places, that the staff have separate tables. And their only participation in the proceedings is an occasional shout to the school diners, 'Keep quiet there'.

One would not insist on all the teachers always dining with pupils, for there is something in the argument that hard-working, nervously exhausted teachers deserve, at lunchtime, the benefit of relaxation that they would be unlikely to get at a pupils' table. But teachers who do not feel that way will be doing the school a service if they sit down at table with their pupils. Embarrassment soon disappears. The conversation becomes relaxed, well mannered, pleasant and civilised. Teachers who have dined with pupils during holidays abroad will know how agreeable the experience can be, and how much the standard of behaviour improves when an adult is with the children at table. The children learn good manners without noticing that they are learning. That this should happen is, nowadays, more important than ever, for so many never have the pleasure of a meal at home with all the family round the table. They feed standing in the kitchen beside the open door of the fridge. They know nothing of the symbolic meaning implicit in the sharing of meat and drink with brothers and sisters.

As the conception of a family is fast disappearing in our society, the schools should boldly step into the breach and confer on their pupils the status of school family membership. The time is past when one can say, 'Their parents should do this or that'. The fact is that many parents have abrogated their duties and certain good things that used to belong to family life, if they are to take place at all, will necessarily have to be done in school. And this is where the House System should be the most effective means of creating a spirit of mutual dependence. Let the two generations, the teachers and the children, sit down in the house dining room in friendly fraternity, old and young crossing, without embarrassment, the generation gap in civilised discussion of matters of common interest.

Perhaps the best sphere for the development of good staff/pupils social relationships is in school activities, clubs, societies, sports teams, etc. These organisations involving voluntary service on the part of staff, outside school hours, have recently been in decline. An increasing number of pupils impelled by the mercenary motives of our time, or more prone than their predecessors to expensive tastes in clothes, drink and entertainment, take part-time employment, making them unavailable for corporate school activities on Saturdays or after four o'clock. We live in a consumer society and the urge to enrich oneself dominates our lives.

Teachers too are less available. Married women rush home on the stroke of four to cook a meal for their husbands and are committed to supermarket shopping expeditions every Saturday morning. Some teachers find specious reasons for withdrawing their voluntary service. There are more promoted posts than ever before and, of course, under the management system, their duties are precisely specified. It is consequently a growing practice to reject any suggestion that one should do any service not stipulated in the official detail of duties. This is a new attitude and a reprehensible one. Some of the responsibility for it lies at the door of the teachers' unions who adopt, from time to time, a work-to-rule policy to pressurise their employers. Those who accept such sordid expedients little realise what they are missing. The colourful and exciting events that take place in the world of school activities, the momentous sports events, the breathtaking stage shows, the adventures of school journeys provide golden memories and rich satisfaction for teachers and pupils. Nor do they seem to know that teachers who work alongside their pupils in after-hours activities acquire influence and respect which spill over in a large measure into classroom relationships. Discipline ceases to be a problem. Once more the gaps between teacher and taught and between the two societies are bridged. Once more those who take part feel themselves a step nearer to the good school society. But the infiltration of restrictive practices into the attitudes teachers take to their duties robs them of the possibilities of the deepest satisfaction. Those who assert that they will do no voluntary extra-curricular service unless they are paid for it have surely never experienced the deep happiness of the sportsfield on a bright autumn morning, the excitement before the curtain rises, the sublimity of the ski-slopes and many another joy. There is no financial equivalent of the spirit that pervades extra-curricular activities. The work is done best when love of the activity is the mainspring. The work is its own reward.

> 'Give all thou canst; High Heaven rejects the lore
> Of nicely calculated less and more.'

Payment for such services would sour the spirit. Vested interests would begin to operate. Activities, neither popular nor valuable, would be foisted on the school for the sake of an instructor's pay-packet; unsuitable, unenthusiastic leaders would squeeze themselves into the extra-curricular field, solely for remuneration, driving the real enthusiast away in disgust; it would be utterly impossible to evaluate the multifarious types of activity or to establish their priority for payment.

No, the right kind of activities supervisor is the enthusiastic volunteer, who kindles a similar enthusiasm in the pupils and establishes a bond of friendship which is likely to be the most enduring thing in the pupil's school experience.

Inter-personal communication between teacher and taught in the classroom is, perhaps, most easily achieved in the practical subjects. The teacher moves amongst his pupils informally, giving each one a certain amount of individual attention. In this situation the teacher has an opportunity to display his own skill, thereby obtaining the respect of the pupils, even their admiration as, for example, in the case of a talented art teacher. The teachers of the academic subjects do not have this advantage. The Physical Education staff are, perhaps, in the strongest position of all. The easy, uninhibited chatter in the changing room, the natural admiration children feel for physical prowess (which, presumably, the PE teacher possesses), the popularity of the subject, the youthfulness of the teachers, such factors combine to create a relaxed and intimate relationship.

In addition to the informal communication which I have been

discussing, classroom discussions and debates are a useful channel of communication. The teacher should be an observer and a listener on these occasions, apart from his duty to encourage the shy ones to speak their minds and to curb the enthusiasm of the over-glib extroverts, who are minded to monopolise the floor. These speech periods have many uses. They are, of course, valuable as another means of finding out what the pupils are thinking about the school. In addition certain civilised notions may be implied: that speakers should be listened to, not shouted down, and that everyone has a right to his opinion (a valuable lesson, surely, in this age of argument by slogan and by demonstration). In these debating and speech periods we should be teaching the art of arguing persuasively but moderately, and the toleration of those who disagree with us. Such principles are part of our democratic heritage and should be part of the ethos of the school. But they are in danger.

All these occasions of communication, involving staff and pupils, make for harmony in the school society; for reducing friction and mis-understanding and bad-tempered confrontations; for developing an awareness of other people's problems; for putting over the message that interests of the community take precedence over those of the individual; for widening the pupils' horizons and nurturing mature, responsible attitudes.

How best may information, instructions, school news, be communicated to the pupils? Some habitually neglect to look at notice-boards.

Some schools produce a daily bulletin, which every registration teacher receives each morning. This document has to be read to the registration class first period. Herein will be found intimations of clubs, societies and sports teams; times of rehearsal and coaching sessions; announcements of school journeys, excursions, theatre visits; compliments and congratulations to those who have brought honour to the school by success in academic and sporting competitions; intimations about visitors to the school; new school rules and warnings about misdemeanours. The bulletin will inform the pupils about staff changes, about the dates of holidays, about the sum raised for charity by the sponsored walk, about the swimming gala, the sports meeting, the choir concert, the school play. It will cover such miscellaneous items as litter, the price of school meals, the times of buses, changes in the timetable, the allotment of rooms for the exams, the Christmas service, applications for university entrance, visits to colleges, school photographs and how to pay for them, graffiti and broken windows and the evils of vandalism in general, the meetings of the Parent-Teacher Association, articles lost and found, school uniform, cycling in the playground and smoking in the bus.

'Here,' as Dryden said, 'is God's plenty.' What, in short, we have here is The School Experience.

It is an admirable system in many ways and should ensure that everything is known by everybody. But no system is foolproof.

For one thing, there are teachers in every staff so utterly dedicated to teaching their subject that they grudge every classroom moment spent in any other way, and they are faintly contemptuous of duties, other than teaching, that emanate from the administrative centre of the school. If they read the bulletin in their classes, they do so in a perfunctory manner; sometimes they even ignore the duty or neglect it. This is serious. Apart from the harm done to administrative arrangements announced in the bulletin, their neglect conveys to the pupils an impression of the unimportance of the bulletin and the information contained therein and, of course, it is an unspoken slight on the head and others who may have been instrumental in drawing it up.

Another weakness of a system that demands the effectual handling of the bulletin by fifty or sixty different registration teachers is that these teachers will vary in their ability to put the announcement over in an interesting and emphatic manner. There will be, alas! teachers who cannot command the attention of their classes — they are regarded as people to whom one does not habitually pay any attention. More numerous than these will be teachers who have given so little thought to their bulletin duty that they have never recognised what an opportunity they have, by their comments on the bulletin, for social education; for deepening the interest of the pupils in the rich, colourful and varied life of the school; for conveying to them some awareness of the obligations that rest on their shoulders as 'citizens of no mean city'. To handle the material in the bulletin satisfactorily, the teacher requires to have some fluency in speech; a wide personal interest in, and a feeling for the value of all the activities of the school; and the ability to explain and illustrate the meaning of new edicts. For, of course, many of the items in the bulletin do require background information and others require a measure of exhortation. No new rule should be promulgated unless the reason for it is given to the pupils. Litter gives extra work to cleaners and blemishes the school's image; broken windows are dangerous and expensive to repair; rules about street crossings may be backed up by accounts of how the problem is tackled in foreign cities. If an appeal for some charity is being announced, a reference to the sufferings of our less fortunate fellow-beings, and the place of compassion in the Christian ethic, will be appropriate. If an outing to a theatre is projected, a word about the romantic experience of theatre-going may stimulate the imagination of the children. A registration teacher who is himself a games player may support an appeal for more sports players by personal reminiscence. When an academic success or a sports achievement is being announced, the reader of the bulletin should add a word of congratulation on his own part if the pupils concerned are in his class. The announcement period should be made an occasion for winning the interest of the children in school affairs, intensifying their feeling of involvement in the community and, generally, presenting the school to their minds as a very exciting place.

Many teachers miss this opportunity. They may lack interest in any happenings outside the orbit of their department. They may be disenchanted ones, long since conditioned to look on their job as drudgery and incapable of imparting any vitality to a school announcement; and reading of the bulletin becomes a mechanical routine.

But even young teachers, who should be enthusiastic about the affairs of the school, may not handle the morning bulletins properly. One wonders if, at any stage, they have received training in how to speak persuasively or forcibly, or even to capture and retain interest by the use of their voice.

It follows, unfortunately, that the practice of making announcements through the bulletin will not be uniformly successful, and the really important announcement will require to be made at the school or house assemblies by someone who knows how to speak to pupils and who believes in the importance of the announcements. No one should be allowed to conduct a school assembly unless he is one who commands attention and respect. The atmosphere of a school assembly should lend impressive force to any announcement made there. I shall deal with these assemblies at a later stage.

It hardly needs saying that announcements made orally in register class or assembly should be repeated on noticeboards for the benefit of absentees or for confirming details.

Notices, announcements, orders, rules, school news, all that falls to be communicated outside the subject departments, all these are the warp and weft of the school life. These items will contribute thoughts and material for conversation in playground, corridor, classroom and common room. A school spirit thrives on noteworthy school happenings, on the heightening of interest in school affairs, on the feeling that what is going on is of some consequence. And so the manner as well as the matter of the communication is of importance. The teacher reading the bulletin should study how he is going to put it across. He should make sure that his voice is audible, that he stresses the important item and explains the obscure. Later he should take the opportunity of discussing the latest news, or the more recent orders, with pupils in his classes, finding out what they think of it all and underlining the assumption that it is very important indeed. This is the time for concerning oneself with the school world outside one's specialist subject.

How much information about the school should be communicated to the pupils? The answer is: more, much more, than they need to know. Let everything of interest be imparted, even although it concerns them only remotely: the new heating system, the identity of some stranger who has appeared in the corridor, the exact state of the school fund, the conference which will necessitate the headmaster's absence for a week. Curiosity should be encouraged — and satisfied. Let much of the talk in playground and corridor be of school affairs, for this will emphasise that all the pupils are partners in the project in virtue of their citizenship.

They will feel flattered, too, by being taken into the confidence of those who manage and govern. (But a word of caution; let the head beware that the pupils do not learn the 'latest news' before the staff.)

Chapter 6

The Headmaster

How far does the quality of a pupil's school experience depend upon the kind of headmaster he has?

The answer depends on the extent of the responsibility he is understood to carry.

The current thinking about school administration veers towards the notion that decision-making in schools should be, largely, democratic; that the staff, or part of the staff, should share in the whole range of decision-making; that, within the school, boards, committees and councils should discuss and settle all issues of policy and corporate decisions should replace the traditional dictatorial pattern.

When the majority of the staff are sensible, co-operative, loyal and actuated by concern for the best interests of the school community, this system works very well. It could well be a safeguard against the consequences of the follies of an eccentric or witless headmaster.

But let us make no mistake about this: the existence of such a democratic system cannot absolve the head from his accountability in terms of his position and of his salary. He must accept responsibility for all that happens in his school just as if the school were a ship and he the captain.

A great deal of nonsense has been talked about this question, both by school inspectors and directors of education who assume, in much that they say, that corporate accountability can co-exist with personal accountability. Parents will just not accept this nor will the pupils.

If a parent has come to the school to complain about the 'grossly unjust' treatment of his son by a teacher in the school, is it suggested that he ought to be satisfied with this reply from the head: 'I quite agree with you that your son was disgracefully treated but my board of studies is responsible for disciplinary policy and I cannot interfere with the methods they have agreed on"? No parent is going to be fobbed off with such an answer. Parents who have serious complaints demand an interview with the head, as they are entitled to do. As for the head, he is a very foolish man if he allows things that he could not himself honestly justify to take place in the school. Parents regard the headmaster as the man with the authority and with the power. And no amount of specious arguments that power is really corporate will convince them otherwise. And this is right. Our society suffers overmuch from anonymous decision-making.

The head is, therefore, thought to be important. And the pupils think so too. Even if there are committees, the focal point of the school government is the headmaster. He is, therefore, part of the children's school experience. What part ought he to play in that experience?

First of all, to put it quite simply, he should be known to them — not just physically as a person hurrying about the school, but as a personality who appears on the rostrum at the school assemblies admonishing and guiding, and as a familiar acquaintance with whom they have had conversations in corridor and playground, as I have already suggested. They will think of him as the one who always seems to be around, and he will impart to them a kind of confidence and a feeling of stability in a society which always seems to be subject to bewildering changes of personnel and full of alarms and excursions as they progress through the varied experiences of the school day.

Those who have been in a school on the occasion of the introduction of a new headmaster will know that to the pupils (and, of course, to the staff) it is a matter of 'deepest consequence' what manner of man the new head is. It is implicitly accepted on all sides — staff, pupils, parents — that his character and his personality will have an influence on the school community. A grey bureaucrat fulfilling his role by remote control from the shelter of a distant office is held in the lowest regard by staff and pupils and parents. Absence of personal magnetism in a head is considered to be a grave defect by staff and pupils and parents. That is a fact. There is no need to argue about it or to prove it. Schools expect their headmasters to be positive men who know their own minds and whose attitudes and values are unequivocal.

A school society is a vortex of positive inter-personal relationships. The elements that form it will vary enormously in value. The head's contribution should be the most potent of all. If it is not, what is he doing there? Why was he preferred to others?

This is not to suggest for one moment that there is, or should be, a standard model for headmastership. While one could list the defects that he must not have, the excellences that he might have are varied and will not all be present in one individual. There will therefore be many different kinds of good headmasters but colourless, neutral types are not in their number.

The pupils like to know where they are with respect to their headmaster. One might be known to be a strict disciplinarian but fair; another a bright man, sparkling with humour, good for morale on a dark December Monday morning; another a moralist, much obsessed with right and wrong; another a sports enthusiast, inspiring the gladiators to illustrious exploits; another an aesthete who had heard 'the golden-snooded muses sing'; another a scholar concerned with precision in speech and writing; another the soul of chivalry, courteous, compassionate. Each of these types could inject his own personal sort of vitality into a school community and the school would be the better for it. But consistency is essential in all he says and does.

It is sad that some headmasters never suspect how much their school community is asking for leadership and for the positive participation of the head in the communal life of the school and how warmly such a response would be welcomed by the children. The education committees, who send such neutral beings to take charge of the minds and spirits of the young, have much to answer for.

Children wish to have a headmaster whom they know, whom they trust and whom they respect. They feel safer and more confident that way. They expect him to be their best guide and adviser and they assume that his decisions will be wise and just. The anonymous head, the neutral head, the diffident head is 'letting them down' and they are quick to identify his shortcomings. They and their parents are contemptuous of the shilly-shallying head who withdraws from the action and lets things take their course.

He must be careful about the image he projects. He must be seen to be just and to be dutiful. Fairness is a value planted deep in the minds of all pupils and it is the basis of school, as it is of every other kind of government. Unreliability and irresponsibility being the most conspicuous faults in the younger generation, it is imperative that the head sets an example of devotion to duty. If he is making strict rules for the conduct of his pupils he must be seen to have strict rules for himself.

This may involve considerable self-discipline on the part of the headmaster, some concealment of his natural inclinations, his human feelings. Do not call it hypocrisy. Self-respect is given to us to help us to do the right thing when we are disinclined to do it. So it is many and many times with the good headmaster.

It is 8.45 on a bleak December morning. The head is in his room contemplating, with no marked enthusiasm, the fifteen-minute school assembly which is due to begin in a few minutes. An irritating cough informs him that a nasty cold is on its way; his appointment diary reminds him of an unpleasant interview with a parent with a serious complaint; a reporter from a tabloid newspaper has just phoned about a playground fight in which someone's head was split and which has the makings of a front-page story. But the head is due to take the morning service and as he meditates on the day ahead he feels no inclination to do any such thing. It occurs to him that he might instruct his faithful deputy to take his place at the rostrum, or if he takes the service himself, to make it a brief perfunctory exercise. He must, however, reject both expedients. He must say to himself, 'Remember who you are. You are head of this school. You frequently adjure your pupils to fulfil accepted obligations. Get on to that rostrum and do your duty.' The headmaster has remembered that he is part of the pupils' school experience.

The head must present to the school a whole range of attitudes, varying according to the day-to-day situations. There are occasions when he must demand complete obedience, even when the issue seems to some to be arguable, when obedience is very inconvenient and there are murmurings of discontent about the edict. On such occasions he must take an early opportunity of counterbalancing the unpopular decision by issuing one about something else, but this time in the nature of a concession or a privilege. The ability to preserve in the life of the school a delicate balance between discipline and freedom, between duty and privilege, between work and play — this is the secret of head-mastering. It is not everyone's gift for it is an instinct — this knowing when to insist and when to yield, when to give and when to take. It is good philosophy too and a good lesson about life that one has to take the rough with the smooth.

That is why the head must, by circulating, keep his finger on the pulse, so that he will recognise the fluctuating moods of the school and know when his pupils have to be brought to heel and when they must be heartened.

Even when he has to adopt the persona of the draconian judge and law-giver, he must remain dignified and not descend to the humiliation of his pupils by screaming at them as if the school were a jungle. A moderate civilised manner of speech must be maintained. A quiet serious tone should always be preferred to a shout or a scream to impress a delinquent. The head's attitude to wrong-doing should display something of the Roman 'gravitas'.

Another concern of the headmaster must be the atmosphere of the school, the feeling in the air, always meaningful to any visitor who has had any experience of schools and who can tell in five minutes whether the school community is in health or sickness. Now this is of immense importance. In a sense the atmosphere of a school is the school experience. The headmaster must keep asking himself the question: 'What does it feel like to be a pupil in this school?' He cannot, of course, enter into the minds of children forty years his junior but he can get a notion of their feelings about the school by going about the premises using his senses, noting what is ugly and what is beautiful, what is disagreeable and what imparts to the mind a feeling of satisfaction or, perhaps, even splendour. He will not neglect sounds or smells. He will keep asking, 'How are the pupils likely to remember this place forty years on?'

Most of the physical features of the building will be beyond his power to change, but he might well achieve a marked effect on the atmosphere by the location of noticeboards, the hanging of pictures, the inscribing of thought-provoking or imaginative quotations at conspicuous places in the corridors and the painting of murals (often the work of senior art students). More important features of the atmosphere are human — what children are allowed to do, what is forbidden. Think of the sounds of school, the echoes of conversations, lively, excited, contentious; footsteps rapid and purposeful; the crowd round the noticeboard where the teams for Saturday's matches are displayed. Then there are the columns on the move, in the beauty of their uniform (how blind the 'progressives', who sneer at school uniform, are to the aesthetic aspect and to the feeling of loyalty and pride and attachment which the uniform symbolises). To see these seemingly endless files moving briskly to unknown destinies calls up a feeling of something visionary. The head should have a feeling for atmosphere which will prompt him to make minor adjustments from time to time. He must hit the right balance of noise in the corridors. There should be a feeling of vitality and happiness, achieved without the element of mindless vociferation of which one is immediately aware in schools where control is uncertain. It is not always easy to draw the line between liveliness and loutishness. Some headmasters adopt the simplistic solution of imposing silence in movement and driving all the pupils into the playground at intervals. This is 'making a desert and calling it peace'. Such schools have no atmosphere at all. There is no reason why civility should not flourish in the corridors and pupils' leisure areas, if the right example is set: welcoming strangers courteously, offering guidance, holding doors open for visitors, the exchange of salutations between pupils and their teachers. The head can promote such practices by his visible example.

The headmaster can contribute to the school experience by his active interest in the school extra-curricular activities. To see him on the touchline gives the player on the pitch the feeling that he and his headmaster are partners in an enterprise which is demanding the best service from both of them. The player will try his hardest for the school and his head will speak to him at the end, sharers in a worthwhile experience. Over and over again the head must make such gestures to his pupils — at concerts, or plays, or debates, or swimming galas, or dancing displays, or general knowledge competitions. Such occasions often provide a momentary 'place in the sun' for pupils who are not academically gifted and the approval or the congratulations of their head recognises their citizenship.

To examine the head's duties to the school at a deeper level, one might say that he should be a source of strength. Not only should he actively encourage and show his appreciation of all who are trying their best, but he should be available for advice or consolation when a pupil is in deep trouble, reinforcing, by his interest and active help, the efforts of the guidance teacher. If the school is a family and he is head of it, those who are unhappy, by reason of poverty or ill health or bereavement, or by the consequence of their wayward conduct, should find him responding to their need. 'I was an hungered and ye gave me meat: I was thirsty and ye gave me drink: I was a stranger and ye took me in; naked and ye clothed me: I was sick and ye visited me: I was in prison and ye came unto me.'

Another duty of the headmaster is to be the person who presents, to the pupils of the school, ethics in unequivocal terms. Let him not be deterred by sneers about middle-class morality or about virtues being merely relative concepts. In our present state of society, a school is a place where children, if abandoned to the numerous unwholesome influences which circulate through the school community, will certainly deteriorate socially and morally unless the school provides a counterweight in the shape of a code of reputable values. For parents do not send their children to school to have their characters ruined and a school that takes a strong line about resisting the spread of vice is doing exactly what most of the parents would wish. And so the school ethic will recommend the good life to the children — honesty; compassion towards the unfortunate; reliability with respect to fulfilling obligations and keeping one's promise; fortitude in the face of misfortune; self-respect as a resistance to the degradation of drinking, drug-taking, glue-sniffing; respect for the persons and properties of others; and refusal to exploit the weak or the vulnerable for one's own advantage. A headmaster who has won the confidence of his pupils by his obvious good will towards them will not be ignored when at assembly, in classroom or in private conversation, he recommends the good life for their consideration.

The extent of the headmaster's influence in the school will depend, largely, on his presence. He will be frequently visible, a permanent, familiar element in the school experience, a source of security and confidence for the young, the immature, the faint-hearted. There should be satisfaction for these pupils in seeing him at assembly, in the dining hall and in the corridors.

But some head teachers (indeed an increasing number) are invisible beings. They are in permanent retreat, immured in their fastnesses remote in the administrative block. The hum and excitement of the real life of the school are, to them, but faint echoes from an irrelevant world.

The architects who conceived the idea of administrative blocks were at fault. The headmaster's room, instead of being so separated, should be located right in the heart of the school, where the eternal files of children pass and repass his door.

The head should think of himself as the centre of a network of personal relationships, not as the head clerk in the documentary school, the school of paper, the school in statistics, the school in working parties' reports, the theoretical school, the impersonal school, the school of shadows and reflections, the school of unreality, the non-school.

The trend in recent years is to belittle the personal element, to disapprove of magnetism in a head or teacher, to treat 'charisma' as a dangerous element. This devaluation of the status of the headmaster, like many other so-styled progressive notions, achieves nothing; it merely robs the school of colour, of idealism, of imaginative undertones, of the feeling that the school experience is a profound and meaningful stage of one's life, and puts nothing in their place. We have fallen into the hands of 'the grey men', the depersonalisers, whose main worry, as they shuffle their papers, is that somewhere in the school, joy, excitement and humour might be disturbing the process of their bleak machinery. 'We are the hollow men,' says T. S. Eliot, 'We are the stuffed men.'

Education is about the growth of human beings to their fullest stature, intellectual, moral, spiritual, and the basic ethic of the school should be the absolute importance of every individual pupil. The image that the head presents must be consonant with this principle. It will determine the example he sets to the staff in civilised converse with the pupils.

Perhaps the most valuable lesson that the head can convey to his staff, by his example, is to talk to all the children in a relaxed, friendly adult way, instead of in the hectoring, authoritative tones, petulant, aggrieved, censorious, testy, peevish, which echo in the memories of all of us from classrooms remote in the years of our childhood. If every teacher in every school in the country could acquire the civilised tone for talking to his pupils, it would do more than any other change to breakdown the us-and-them hostility which activates the young rebels against society.

One cannot over-emphasise the importance of what the head says to, or in the hearing of, his pupils. What he has to say at assembly (there will be more of this later) must be carefully considered and delivered with professional vocal technique. (Should heads take lessons in elocution?) Off-the-cuff judgements instantly pronounced are fraught with danger. What is said should be delivered in clear and moderate language, with obviously serious intent and not without warmth.

Another matter that the head should concern himself with, closely and constantly, is the status of his Sixth Year, or of the Fifth if there is no Sixth. Something will be said later about the position the Sixth should occupy in the school community and the type of service that should be required of them. The school has failed, abysmally, to impart its social and moral philosophy to the senior pupils unless they have acquired commitment and loyalty. If they do not feel that way about the school, if they are cynical, unresponsive or even derisive about the affairs of the school, then the head has been deficient in leadership and is clearly unfit for the position he holds. One is depressed at the number of teachers, and even headmasters, who have never acquired the right approach to the senior pupils. These young people are crying out for guidance and encouragement and sensitive about infringements of their dignity and their status. They may be silent but will not forgive those who thoughtlessly humiliate them by censuring them in the presence of juniors or watch, gestapo-like, the happenings in the senior common room or who are ready to withdraw, in the interests of so-called discipline, the little amenities and privileges the possession of which should distinguish them from the younger pupils. How pitifully small are the privileges, the granting of which satisfies these hesitant adolescents. And how reluctant are some headmasters to grant them these.

The good headmaster will build up a trustful relationship with his senior pupils. He will meet them frequently and informally. He will sometimes join them in their common room for coffee. He will not

turn a deaf ear to their criticisms and complaints. Where proposed
innovations are likely to have a significant effect on the school
population, he will listen to what they may have to say. He will have
them close at hand, inter-mixed with the staff on social occasions,
ushering, receiving guests, conducting visitors round the school. No
occasion in which they might be given some position of responsibility
should be neglected. He should not forget their dignity, even when one
or more of them have fallen from grace and some disciplinary measures
are necessary. A serious reprimand from the head will meet most cases,
a reprimand given in the presence of the offender's fellow-pupils but
never of younger pupils.

If the head makes the Sixth his special concern, a stable trustful
relationship will develop and its influences will be felt throughout the
school.

The headmaster will approach these young men and women as
responsible adults, their reliability being taken for granted. This
confidence will be conveyed by the civility with which he addresses
them. Their status in the school will be seen to be one of partnership,
not of inferiority. If the head's integrity and his commitment to the
service of his pupils are not in doubt, he need not fear a cynical
response. The Sixth will be his best advocates out there in the pupils'
world and the school's most convincing ambassadors in the world
beyond the gates.

I shall return to the importance of the Sixth later in this volume. It is
vital. The spirit of the whole school is conditioned by the example of
the Sixth, their service and their loyalty. Many teachers seem to be
unaware of this. And so in many schools the Sixth is but the withered
branch of the tree, undernourished and neglected by staff who barely
seem to notice them in the corridor.

Let the nurture of these senior pupils be the head's special concern. If
he does not attend to this, it is unlikely that anyone else will.

The old-fashioned word 'leadership' may still best describe the role
of the headmaster. And as a leader he will be identified with every
aspect of the school's life and history. He should be seen to be involved
in the school's honour and disgrace, in its achievements and failures,
just as Donne said we were all involved in mankind. If someone wins
credit for the school by some academic or sporting achievement or if a
letter of thanks comes in with appreciation of some courteous service
performed by the pupils, it should be commented on in the school
assembly in terms that suggest that the honour is reflected on all, staff,
pupils and head. If there has been disgrace, shoplifting, violence or

drunkenness, it will be made clear that all, head as well as pupils, have suffered devaluation.

When some such disagreeable incident occurs, perhaps involving unwelcome publicity, there will be no evasion of the issue, no sweeping under the carpet. The head must be seen to be accepting responsibility for it. (He must act upon the harsh assumption that there are no bad schools or bad pupils, only bad headmasters.) He should face any adverse publicity that may be incurred, make frank statements, if statements are appropriate, honestly admit errors if errors there have been and should never meanly shuffle off the responsibility on the shoulders of some defenceless subordinate, less able than he to endure the burden of whatever unpleasant repercussions the incident may have occasioned.

The identification of the head with his school will be emphasised by his present at school occasions, games, concerts, debates, operas, plays, parents' meetings, journeys and outings etc. When the ordinary business of the day, involving its twelve hundred pupils, is over and the majority are at home, there will often be a group participating in a school occasion: a team going out to win a place in a final, the gym team putting on a display, the orchestra performing at a carol service. During the time of that after-hours activity or event, those taking part are The School. For the time of the performance of the event, the school's reputation is entirely and solely in their hands. (They must be made to understand this.) His presence will reinforce the conception that for the moment this group is the school.

And so if one has done some service to the state, or added lustre to the school's image, let that pupil be summoned to the head's room and warmly thanked. In many cases a mention at school assembly will be warranted.

Headmasters should be specially watchful lest any service, however small, done by a disadvantaged child should go without a proper tribute. The cause of much of delinquency is just that the malefactor has never in his life earned a word of praise or a ray of limelight and takes to violence or vandalism as a compensation, just for a time to be conspicuous — if only in a notorious role. If every one of the pupils, particularly the dullest ones, would, for 'one crowded hour' of his school life, be publicly praised or congratulated, a significant improvement in behavioural standards would be apparent. Let such recognition of even small services be a constant obligation.

The headmaster should note the changing moods of the school community. When that community has a common experience, a common emotion will prevail. An extreme form of this may have its dangers — we are all familiar with the mass hysteria of, for example, football crowds when a collectively experienced mood intensifies with dangerous potentiality. All who have ever been in a school know that Monday morning is an entirely different experience from Friday afternoon. The last half-day of the week has its special euphoria, a carefree, buoyant, expectant feeling from which no pupil is immune.

Each of many events can evoke its own peculiar mood in pupils and, in many cases, in staff: the beginning and the end of examinations; the opening and the closing of the term or of the session; the approach of a colourful extra-curricular event, like a fête or a school show, or an excursion, or a sports day; a competitive event like a football final or a general knowledge contest; the announcement of a half holiday or an early closure (such a small thing).

The mood, of course, may be despondent: the imminence of the examinations; a tightening of discipline; the withdrawal of some long-established and highly esteemed privilege; the closing of a common room; a wholesale failure in an external exam; the abandonment of some widely practised school activity; the departure of a well-loved person, headmaster, teacher or janitor; a wholesale punishment — any one of these may cast a temporary shadow over the minds of many children, not to speak of greater calamities like the death of a pupil or teacher. Events outside the school may affect the prevailing mood: the result of a cup-tie in which the local team was involved; a pop concert anticipated or recalled in excited conversation; a sensational television programme the previous evening.

The wise head will concern himself with the emotional temperature of the school as he reads it day by day. He may find occasion to capitalise on it or modify it. If the mood is dismal, he may counteract it by some more cheerful announcement, some pleasing concession on a minor issue, some slight and interesting variation in normal procedure. The announcement of changes that might affect the feeling of the pupils should be cautiously timed, welcome announcements balanced with disagreeable ones; some new freedom offered as a counter-weight to some new restriction; some privileges given in exchange for a strict insistence on duties. Let no one think that this aspect of school government is trivial. It is the secret of school government — the maintenance of the equilibrium between discipline and freedom, between obligation and one's personal inclinations.

To preserve an equable atmosphere, some cheerfulness should be contrived to counterbalance the gloom of the dark winter season; and conversely when an abandoned, festive mood prevails, there should be a reminder, to all concerned, that routine studies must not be put in jeopardy by prolonged junketing.

The head will contribute something to the mood of the school by helping to form attitudes. Every school will experience, at some time or other, unfavourable press reports — publicity given perhaps to some act of vandalism or violence or a public revelation of disreputable practices, drugs, glue-sniffing, drinking. This will, naturally, affect the morale of the whole school. The head will not bury his head in the sand, for by so doing he will not prevent widespread discussion, in the playground and in homes, injurious to the school's reputation. If the reports have been exaggerated he will correct these. He will put into perspective damaging judgements that may be made outside. He will convey to the pupils that he shares their concern about the tarnishing of the school's good name and he will call on them to repair the damage by fresh efforts to practise virtue. Where defeat has been suffered he may well pluck some consolation or even glory from the embers nor will he omit to remind them that there is always another day, recalling perhaps the famous ending of the Victorian novel: 'The sun has set,' said Mr Inglesant, 'but it will rise again.'

Should greater calamity befall the school family, such as the death of one of its members, this should be recognised as the school's portion of the tragic lot of humanity. Some simple ceremony should bring the school to pause, even fleetingly, on the threshold of the unknowable.

The conception of emotional education is worthy of the consideration that it seldom receives. It is, of course, the basis of the aesthetic subjects, music, art, poetry, drama, dancing and, to some extent, of the crafts, but it is relevant to the reactions of pupils to real events in the life of the school. When serious things are encountered, illness, death, the plight of the handicapped, the sufferings of children at the hands of their fellows, cruelty to animals, etc., it is the duty of the head to convey to the pupils a civilised and compassionate reaction and to show the impropriety of cynical and derisive responses — the black humour, prevalent in our subcultures, with which our children are too well acquainted.

Some of the emotional phases in the life of a school may be trivial and ephemeral but these must not necessarily be neglected, for any community as closely packed as a school is a dangerous field, never secure from the possibility of unpredictable explosions. Some pupils will get very excited about a cup-tie replay on a Wednesday afternoon (should the school be released early to allow them to attend?); the proposal to turn a disco hall into a venue for bingo (let's get up a petition); a gang fight which involved many of the pupils the previous evening (let us get our own back on the pupils of the rival school tomorrow night). The head should know about all this and have something to say, a decision to make, and to carry out.

Most dangerous for the school and the head may be a report in the media of trouble in other schools, protest marches, sit-ins, strikes. Striking is a daily feature of industrial life and it is a fever, highly infectious.

Precedents are not lacking for militants who wish to stir up 'industrial trouble' in a school and they will get plenty of support from pupils' pseudo-political bodies ('pseudo' because they have generally been initiated by adult extremist bodies). News of a strike or demonstration in one school soon gets around and others will follow if a grievance can be found or invented. The head will pre-empt such eruptions, with all their disagreeable publicity and internal disturbance, by making himself conversant, well in advance, with any grievance that would be likely to cause this type of action. He should be more ready to deal with such a crisis if he is conversant with the issues that might possibly spark off a revolt or demonstration (and, again, it is a question of liaison or 'ear to the ground'). It is his duty to present to the dissidents a sensible balanced point of view, whether it is about the wearing of slacks by girls in winter, the programme for the school party or the cancellation thereof or homework regulations or school dinners. He should always gauge the strength of feeling in the school about any such issue and should certainly have the expertise to present the matter to the pupils without prejudice or stuffy humbug. If things are not going his way, he must decide whether to withdraw as gracefully as he can, accept a compromise (usually the best solution) or stand immovably on principles. He must recognise that he cannot be the complete autocrat and much will depend on the nature of the relations he has built up with his pupils. The amount of loyalty and co-operation he can command will vary according to the nature of his personality. If, in addition to being clearly a man dedicated to the service of his school, he is reasonable, moderate, and fluent enough to put his case in terms that will convey his concern for the best interests and the reputation of the school, he will have nothing to fear from any militants, particularly if they are actuated by doctrinaire notions from some extreme adult political party.

The headmaster who regularly takes the school into his confidence, explains his own difficulties and the factors which he has to consider before making a decision (most of these factors that they, the pupils, have never thought of) will generally carry the pupils with him. On the other hand, a graceful withdrawal on some not too important issue, now and again, with an admission to the school that he, the head-master, is not infallible, will do him no harm at all. It will probably heighten the respect in which he is, or should be held, and help to avoid opposition about some question which he regards as more important. But it all adds up to this — that he should, one way or another, know what the school thinks and feels and how strong is the feeling, and thus he will have his own position clarified long before an issue becomes public.

I have been arguing for direct relations between head and pupils over and above the more formal structure of delegation, reaching down to them through mechanically operated chains of command. As the year goes on he should attempt to get to know as many names as is humanly possible. In a large school he cannot know them all, and many heads will argue that if he cannot know them all, it is not worth while knowing any of them. But it is amazing just how many one can get to know if one tries. Let the pupils wear badges with their names. Every time the head makes a personal impact by naming a pupil correctly, in the child's mind a new and quite stimulating relationship will have sprung up. The pupil has found an identity within the school which may originate a strong affection previously not experienced. The head's acquaintanceship with his pupils will widen notably if he accompanies them on outings, journeys and educational holidays or visits to an outdoor centre. Mutual understanding and friendship develop and the facade of caution, behind which the pupil shelters in his dealing with teachers in school, is dropped, to the considerable advantage of both sides.

Chapter 7

The Head Teacher and the Staff

The key to the creation of a happy school community is, of course, a sense of being part of a team, each component working for the good of the whole. Clearly it will be easier to convey this ideal to the scholars if they see it significantly at work on the part of the staff. Pupils would be the first to notice if it were not there. They know well enough which of their teachers support school activities and seem to be willing to lend a hand wherever help is required. The more teachers there are on the staff of the type I describe, versatile, resourceful, co-operative people who are ready to contribute to any school enterprise, even if it is not specifically within their remit, the better for the school; and well the pupils know it.

But it does not always work out like that. Several factors militate against it.

The number of promoted posts in secondary school has escalated in recent years and there is no harm in that. The mistake that is being made about these posts is that their duties have been too exactly specified. There has, consequently, been a tendency for the holders of such positions to adhere rigidly to the duties defined for them in the terms of their appointment and to refrain from any other service not so specified, as for example involvement in corporate activities. Such teachers might well argue that they are too fully occupied with their official duties to undertake any unofficial ones. But this argument is not always acceptable. Needs of schools vary. A school of one thousand pupils in a slum area would get exactly the same establishment of guidance staff as one in a socially superior district. The teacher in the former area would be overworked; the one in the latter would have a comparatively easy time.

Again, a school might have a special problem as, for example, a racially mixed population or a remotely scattered catchment area, or a long tradition of truancy, or the need for after-hours activities to combat endemic vandalism — and such aspects would not be mentioned in anyone's terms of appointment though they were crying out for attention. And since they were not mentioned it might be hard for the headmaster to persuade any of his promoted staff to give them their attention.

Again, no matter how comprehensively the duties of a promoted teacher are defined, important matters will be omitted. Unforeseen happenings, new habits and new attitudes enter the stream of the school's life and affect its atmosphere. But if it has become habitual for a teacher to say 'That is not my business — it is not in my contract — I'm not paid for doing that', some entirely undesirable feature may have taken root in the social life of the school, disregarded by most of the staff.

It is sad to observe how the amount of service, of an extra-curricular nature, done by teachers has declined in recent years during the very period when posts carrying responsibility payment were increasingly available. Any reader who doubts this should compare the number of school teams out on Saturday morning with the position ten years ago.

A new approach to conditions of service and job specification is required. A solution might be found in a system similar to that accepted in the Army with respect to commissioned rank. The role of an officer is not defined in other than general terms because he may be asked to accept any role or any task demanded by the immediate situation. He must, therefore, be versatile, resourceful and prepared to play a part in a new situation or a new emergency.

So it should be with the promotion of teachers. Each school should be allotted so many posts of responsibility proportionate to its roll but the duties should be unspecified. The person appointed should be prepared to accept duties pertinent to the special needs of that particular school and should also be ready to accept new roles demanded by new or changing circumstances. Such a system would bring about an improvement in the quality of the promoted staff, for it would be accepted that one of the main criteria for appointment would be wide versatility. Another would be resourcefulness in respect of new assignments. The current defence of the legalists and the un-imaginative plodders, 'I was not trained to do this' or 'I am not paid to do this', would no longer be tenable.

Another advantage of this more flexible system of assignment of duties would be that it would be possible, within a school, for the promoted teacher to be assigned duties appropriate to his talents, interests or circumstances. One teacher, noted for his precision and for his patience, might take over the direction of registration in a large school with an alarming truancy problem. An unmarried teacher, with an unquenchable enthusiasm for games, might accept responsibility for organising the playing fields on Saturday afternoons. Another man, whose domestic circumstances made it advantageous for him to leave school early on several afternoons, might be accorded this privilege in return for managing activities at lunchtime. A teacher who lived locally and was president of the Rotary Club might accept responsibility for some branch of public relations. The policy would be that holders of promoted posts, instead of having their services confined to the clauses contained in the contract at the time of their appointments, would be expected to accept a succession of roles, some peculiar to the particular school, others emerging from time to time in its ever-changing and ever-developing life.

For the danger is that a compact, precisely structured system of management may create the illusion that once the master-plan has been put into operation, the machine will run itself. Every eventuality seems to have been catered for, but the unpredicted thing happens. It is nobody's business. It may lie out there somewhere in the no-man's land between the chains of command. A subject has suddenly become popular or unpopular or is in swift decline; absenteeism among fourth year girls on Friday afternoons is soaring; pupils, for no obvious reason, have started to frequent an old folk's shelter in the park; ticket sales for the concert are not going well; pupils have stopped using the school library at intervals; some well-behaved pupils in first year are showing symptoms of school aversion; several footballers have been ordered off in recent games; some school rugby players have started playing for a hard-drinking adult team; the head of Art has fallen out with the head of Technical and as a result there is to be no scenery for the school play. Such incidents and developments may be danger signals or flashpoints. Many of them could have been cleared up if a teacher, close to the situation, forgot his work specification and used his initiative. A wise head will encourage his staff to operate outside their remit. Such encouragement will underline the general principle that the overall health of the school community is everyone's business.

There are, then, likely to be some matters which have not been specified in anyone's delegated work load merely because they have not been anticipated. There are others which should not be delegated at all. Difficult interviews with indignant parents, delicate diplomacy to reconcile clashing personalities at staff or pupil level, rumours of scandal ripe for the attention of the media — such things demand top-level handling and no headmaster should shirk them on the plea that they are the business of one of his subordinates. It is, unhappily, true that some problems are delegated largely because of their unpleasantness.

Now the headmaster must be prepared to accept irksome and worrying loads. That is what he is paid for. That is the meaning of responsibility. If experience, judgement, diplomacy, courage and probity are the qualities required, then the head is surely the one who has these in the greatest measure. Else, why is he there? There is more to his job than slitting open letters in the morning and distributing the contents among his various subordinates.

Discipline is a dangerous area where delegation may lead to unpleasant consequences, and head-on confrontation between a teacher and a pupil should never be left to be settled by a subordinate. The teacher may have committed himself to some unjustifiable course of action without room for manoeuvre; the pupil may be less at fault than the teacher. A solution may require the most delicate diplomacy. Two attitudes must be reconciled; the pupil must not go away thinking that there is no justice in the school (for the head is the source of justice), but a verdict unfavourable to the teacher might weaken his authority. The head must call on all his experience to contrive a compromise solution which will be face-saving for the teacher and not notably unjust to the pupil. It can usually be done but not without an interval of a day or two to allow temperatures to cool. The diplomacy required to achieve reconciliation, by both parties attaining a more responsible view of the incident, is a necessary component of a headmaster's armoury. Its importance can hardly be overstated. It is regrettable that so many heads are blind to the explosive potentialities of these situations — defiance, ill temper, hardening of positions, suspensions, involvement of parents, press publicity — all following because the head, however expert he might be with the management system, lacks the essential ability to arbitrate from a base of sympathy, patience and experience.

All the head's experience should be at the disposal of his staff as they carry out their allotted duties. He must be a source of strength, especially to the younger members. He may have sometimes to rescue them from pitfalls and dilemmas, even if these are of their own making. He must keep himself in touch with the decision-making of his various subordinates. He may be obliged, if hesitantly, to suggest a modification of some policy or procedure or the arrest of a dangerous trend. The feelings, the standing, the pride of a loyal well-meaning colleague may be involved. The operation may demand diplomacy, timing, judgement of character, so that the teacher concerned may be unaware of the prompting and may, indeed, imagine that he is correcting the dangerous trend on his own initiative.

Such a process will be all the easier if there is close rapport between the head and his staff. Just as he must have continuous conversational links with his pupils, so with his staff. In recent years it has become increasingly common for the head to keep himself to his room, communicate with the teachers by circular, memorandum or letter and even insist that a member of staff can have a consultation with the head only if he makes an appointment some time a day or two ahead. This is management run mad.

The relationship between head and staff should be of such cordiality that interviews would take place without formality or fuss. If it is assumed that every teacher has some duty, extra to his teaching, some extra-curricular work or a special assignment, it is proper that he should report and discuss. And the head, on his part, should actively seek opportunities for conversation with his colleagues on each individual's special field of interest or of duty. The relevant questions may then be asked and answered and a much appreciated word of encouragement given.

Harmony in a staff will depend largely on how far they feel that they are involved in decision-making and in forming the policies by which the school is governed.

There is an obvious reluctance nowadays on the part of head-masters to consult their staffs through the medium of the staff meeting. This is largely through fear that their authority in the school may be challenged by opposition from voluble militants, primed with shibboleths emanating from some union splinter group, thirsting for a showdown on some divisive issue. But no head need fear such confrontations if the measure under discussion is clearly in the interests of the school society as a whole. It is hard for even the most rabid and fluent school politician to hold his own against a headmaster whose integrity, sincerity and dedication are not in dispute.

How far should the government of the school be a democratic process? There is no precise answer to that question.

You will find schools where autocratic status for the headmaster is assumed or imposed. His favourite phrase is 'my school' delivered smugly or arrogantly. It recurs when reprimanding delinquent pupils. 'You will not behave like that in *my* school.' The image such heads present, to both their staff and pupils, is one of vanity, intolerance, and an air of infallibility. His character does not improve with the passage of time. His assistants feel depressed and frustrated as the atmosphere of the school is soured by the corruption that is said to accompany absolute power.

At the other extreme the view prevails, in some quarters, that the head should be no more than a chairman at a variety of staff meetings and committees. But has this interpretation of his function any legal validity? As long as the word 'responsibility' is used in contracts, the person concerned must, surely, be accountable for all that happens in his area of surveillance. If something goes wrong he cannot escape the consequences by transferring the blame to some committee of the staff. If inspectors and local authorities are in earnest about democracy in school government, the headmaster should be designated simply as 'Chairman of the school board of studies but without any personal decision-making powers'.

'Corporate responsibility' is, of course, a popular contemporary postulate. In bureaucratic governmental departments, national and local, it is well nigh impossible to find out who makes the decisions that govern our lives. No individual will openly accept responsibility for an unpopular decision and none is available to face criticism or to answer complaints. Another disadvantage of corporate responsibility is that it makes for inefficiency and indolence. An individual, aware that he will not be called personally to account for errors and failures, may not take the trouble to ensure that errors and failures will not occur.

In a general way every member of the staff should be able to make a significant contribution to the policy of the school and should be able, at certain levels, to make decisions without necessarily consulting higher authority. But the headmaster, presumably having more to contribute in respect of the personal qualities in virtue of which he received his appointment, should make greater contributions to the processes of policy-making and decision-making than the others.

An unfortunate aspect of present-day management is that the head may have been selected for promotion by reason of the extent and variety of his personal assets and then when he takes over his promoted posts, the area for exercising his talents is markedly reduced. But the vitality of the school community will depend on the extent to which head and staff give their all, for education is, essentially, the process by which one mind enriches another.

There are many qualities which a head may possess in greater abundance than his staff. He may have a flair for administration, an instinct for knowing what will work and what will not; in the curricular field his experience may tell him what are the potentialities of each subject as contributing to the ideal of the all-round human being; he may have a shrewd mind for appraising character, personality and ability in his staff; he himself may be a born teacher, able to show others how to face and handle a class; he may really understand children, know how to win their co-operation and loyalty; similarly he may have a gift for handling adults and for maintaining harmony in his staff; he may be versatile and wide ranging in his interests, resourceful in developing the extra-curricular side; he may possess the quality of leadership which can inspire staff and pupils to accept difficult objectives; he may be a fluent speaker, able to explain the reasons for and the implications of his policies lucidly and persuasively; he may be a person of great physical stamina, nervous energy and drive so that vitality will flow from him to the school; he may have a broad vision of education, embracing a wide range of objectives and the judgement for settling priorities in respect of these; he may have the character that drives him on in face of failures and setbacks and maintains morale in those around him.

Every head, in my view, should have some of these qualities in abundance and should not be entirely devoid of any one of them. He should be in a position to employ all that he has in the service of the school, uninhibited by theories of corporate responsibility.

It follows that he should have much more say in decision-making than his colleagues.

If for no other reason he alone is in a position to appraise the rights, difficulties and prevailing conditions of the various departments in the school, to balance conflicting vested interests and to establish proper priorities. He possesses fuller information about staff and pupils than anyone else and about the efficiency of his various departments. No other person in the school can possibly have access to all the data relevant to making policy decisions.

The head, too, is the continuing presence. He has seldom any interest in further promotion and his term in the school is likely to be longer than those of most of his colleagues. His view of the school will have a wider perspective. If mistakes are made about important issues of policy, he is the one who will have to live with them.

The head, also, will see the history of the school as a continuing stream with an identifiable permanent shape, augmented from time to time by new tributaries but giving comfort to all that pass through by presenting an image of permanence in an unstable world. The head will be the stable factor, moderating the speed of change and monitoring new developments by his extensive knowledge of the school's history and his concern for its long-term interests.

In moulding the staff into a harmonious team, the social aspect is important. It should be customary for morning coffee to be dispensed only in a large, comfortable staff common room, where friendly and fruitful inter-personal and inter-departmental relations may develop. In a good school community people should be aware of and interested in what others are doing. A shared social area also aids communication and an informal chat there will be less time consuming and perhaps more productive than a written communication or a telephone conversation. One of the main evils of the large school is departmental fragmentation, induced by the use of the department bases as social centres. The parochial attitude engendered by separate subject units should be replaced by a fuller, wider consciousness of the obligations the school may demand from each of its members.

A sensible head will also encourage staff socialising outside school hours, with staff dinners, theatre nights, golf outings, musical groups, football and badminton clubs, anything, in short, which promotes friendships and a family feeling.

It is important that on social occasions, professional ranking should be disregarded. Teachers who have enough interest to appear at evening school functions should be free to use the refreshment table in the headmaster's room and rub shoulders with the official guests. They must never be allowed to think themselves unimportant; their presence should be appreciated..

A headmaster should welcome opportunities for informal conversations with his teachers, not only to find out what is in their minds but to spread his own philosophy abroad. If head and teachers are in close rapport the marked individual differences in attitudes to pupils may be smoothed out and pupil-teacher relationships acquire desirable stability. This is particularly true in the sphere of discipline generally and of punishment.

Teachers in Scottish schools have an extraordinary amount of freedom with respect to judging disciplinary incidents and imposing punishments. Many heads are gravely at fault in not knowing or not wishing to know how members of the staff are dealing with misdemeanours, serious or trivial. It should be one of the head's main functions to spell out to his staff, particularly the inexperienced members, a sensible, moderate, just method of imposing discipline. The insensitivity of many teachers to the ethics of discipline is disturbing. The use of sarcasm to which the pupil under attack has no means of reply; the quite dishonourable practice of encouraging pupils to inform against their fellows in respect of not too serious offences; the 'third degree' approach, by which the teacher falsely pretends that he has information which will incriminate the accused pupil, in the hope of extorting a confession; the imposition of mass punishment because one single culprit has not confessed; the maintaining of hostility towards an offender after that person has been punished; the assumption that the head is bound to support the teacher in any head-on collision with a pupil over crime and punishment. On all such matters the head's duty is to give clear direction and, at the same time, to know whether his directions are being complied with.

One will never achieve complete uniformity in the methods used to maintain good order and respect for rules. There will always be hard teachers and soft teachers and such differences may contribute welcome variety to the patchwork of school experiences. But inconsistency in dealing with clear breaches of school rules may do great harm. The same offence is condoned by some teachers, severely dealt with by others. Judgement may be passed without proper investigation. Prejudice or favouritism may affect the decision. Nothing in the day-to-day life of the school alienates the pupils more than what they regard as injustice. It harms morale and destroys the confidence the pupils ought to have in those in authority. Indeed when a pupil is asked for his opinion of his headmaster, the first question which it occurs to him to ask is 'Is he fair?'.

Disciplinary powers, of course, have to be delegated but it is the head who has to explain and defend decisions and actions, in this field, to complaining parents. On such occasions, the reputation of the school is involved.

Every head has found himself in the position of defending a subordinate's action when he really thought that the colleague had been unwise, rash or downright irresponsible. He should pre-empt such episodes by initial clarification of the teacher's disciplinary functions. To the novice he should give warnings about pitfalls arising from over-hasty judgements, or prejudices, or over-reacting through ill temper. A calm, unhurried, judicial approach to misdemeanours should be emphasised. Some err in threatening too much; others in not carrying out threats that have been made. The cultivation of the friendly rebuke for trivial faults is generally achieved by experience. Young teachers should be advised to seek advice from more experienced colleagues about potentially dangerous classroom situations before these have come to a head. The fruits of the experience of the headmaster and the senior teachers should be passed on, as occasion demands, to the lower echelons. The flow of helpful advice, to those who need it, will be most useful when it comes informally. A friendly chat in a comfortable corner of a cheerful common room will be the most effective medium for such communication, rather than the 'memorandum for the attention of all probationers', or a semi-judicial admonition in the headmaster's austere retreat.

The head who dons a cloak of infallibility or of authoritarianism, in advising young colleagues, is more likely to provoke antagonism than to inspire respect. I wonder how many heads realise how much depends on the image they present to probationers on this first encounter. The head must be at his best, earnest, considerate, unpretentious. The young teacher must feel that he is welcome, trusted, accepted as a partner in the team.

No matter how busy a head may be, some part of every day should be devoted to visiting classrooms. In this way he becomes familiar with the strengths and weaknesses of his staff and finds occasions for encouragement or advice. An experienced head gauges the atmosphere of a classroom almost before he has entered it. (A moderate amount of noise may mean that the teacher is absent from the room. A greater din may indicate that a certain Mr X is actually there and officially in charge.) Such a head will detect, in a moment, the quality of the classroom atmosphere; orderliness, purposefulness, interest, respect, cordiality, good humour, tension, fear, boredom, derision or contempt, and so on. When he senses trouble, he will have a number of options: advice to the teacher, consultation with the head of the department, more frequent visits to the classroom, a change in the timetable, a review of the teacher's suitability for various kinds of work. What he must not do is to interfere with the situation immediately, thus humiliating the teacher and damaging his status in the eyes of the pupils. Such situations are usually too complex to be dealt with in that arbitrary manner. Often only a palliative is possible, such as the transfer of a few pupils to another section. Encouragement may take the form of reminiscence of his own early 'salad days' when he was 'green in judgement' and the assurance that the first year is the worst and things will look entirely different the following year. Let him never forget that the unruly class is only part of the problem; the question of the teacher's morale is of equal importance. Sustenance rather than reproof is the prior requirement.

If communication between the head and his staff should be frequent and friendly, as I have argued, the head's relations with the senior promoted staff, deputy, assistant heads and heads of school, should be intimate and continuous. Ideally the head should have two offices: a small private study, to which he may withdraw when he requires to work without interruption and for confidential interviews; and a larger outer office which he should share with the senior staff. The whole group would use the room as a cloakroom, coming together every morning and being there, very frequently, during the day. It would be a conclave in continuous session to monitor the ever-changing shape of the proceedings of the school. When an unpredicted problem arose there would be several responsible, experienced people together to take a decision about it, and, in serious crises, to maintain the morale of one another. As for new emerging policies, every aspect of an issue would be under examination in free, friendly dialogue, moving towards a decision by consensus, a firm, clear, unequivocal conclusion stripped of all irrelevancies and with priorities indisputably established. In comparison with this prolonged on-going conference, unimpeded by procedural restraints or durational pressures, the conventional formal board of studies might appear to be a somewhat blunt instrument of government.

In this unofficial cabal, the deputy headmaster may hold a special position. Perhaps he has been on the staff for a very long time, possibly longer than the head himself, and the need to give his all to the service of the school has become so much second nature to him that he would thank no colleague for lightening his servitude. He loves the school and watches jealously over her health and her honour. He carries in his mind an irreplaceable store of knowledge, of families, school customs and traditions; he has invaluable contacts in the community; he has an intuitive awareness of significant changes in the school atmosphere. A new headmaster, fortunate enough to have such a man as his deputy, would make a working relationship with him his first priority and would accord to him a status in the school little short of his own. Such a man provides a frame of reference for all new projects and policies and is a guardian of good customs and living traditions.

Chapter 8

Guidance and Social Education

If one of the functions of the school is to promote socially acceptable standards of conduct and to try to remove causes of discontent and unhappiness in individual members of the school family, then the guidance teachers (sometimes designated house masters and mistresses) are key people. Their duties are manifold but the most important of these must, necessarily, be concerned with the problem pupils: the emotionally disturbed, the psychologically unstable, the socially deprived, the frustrated, demoralised academic rejects, the loners, the drop-outs, the rebels, the citizens of the school's alternative society. Their task is 'to rescue the perishing' but, of course, it often seems quite impossible. The origin of a pupil's failure to adjust to the school society may lie in psychological experiences in early childhood or in an irremediably disturbed domestic background. But even when the case is apparently hopeless, there will be phases of intermission when the pupil may respond to friendly gestures and briefly experience at school happiness that he does not know at home. For he is one of the school family and in a Christian family one does not readily run short of patience and forgiveness.

But the break-up of the school into two societies is a problem about which something can be done, for it is a phenomenon that takes place before our very eyes in the latter part of the second year, when a sizeable part of the school population experience the moment of truth about its academic inadequacy.

The guidance master must concentrate on identifying the moment of secession and in this he must have the co-operation of every teacher of a second year class. The signs are there for all to see: a deterioration in behaviour, an abandonment of school uniform, a change of friends, a growing truculence in speech, a rebellious attitude with regard to discipline previously accepted.

The guidance master must move in immediately. His task is to persuade the pupil that he is a valued member of the school community and that the school has something of value to offer him. The master, himself, must exemplify the school's concern by his own earnest and sympathetic way of speaking to the pupil and he must meet and converse with him frequently. If any success is to be gained, the co-operation of colleagues is essential. If the pupil has achieved even a little success in a subject, then the teacher of that subject must express continued interest and appreciation. And participation in school activities may be a lifeline. If the pupil has the slightest interest in, or ability at, a sport, he should be persuaded to play it with the school club; and a large stage show, with a huge chorus, should, properly, offer a place in the sun for those who have failed to find it in the academic world. It follows that, if this line of approach is to have any success, the guidance master must have the co-operation of other teachers, those who organise games or produce stage shows or who run hobbies clubs, or who take children to the outdoor centre or on school journeys. Too often such organisers of activities concentrate on the most capable pupils, for if one is organising an activity the main pleasure is in seeing the thing, whatever it is, well done. Consequently one often finds that a few bright, versatile pupils capture the limelight in several activities, while hundreds of the less gifted take no part at all.

Now if the guidance master cannot persuade the organisers of activities to give a chance to some of the problem children on the brink of transferring themselves to the alternative society, it will be incumbent upon him to find the answer within his own house. The house should have its own range of hobbies, sports teams and sports leagues, competitions, money-raising activities, stage shows, all designed, primarily, to offer a centre of interest to pupils who are beginning to think of themselves as school rejects.

Much may be achieved, too, by creating posts of responsibility connected with the day-to-day running of the house. The perform-ance of these duties should bring the pupil frequently into contact with the house master, presenting opportunities for friendly encourage-ment.

If there are house assemblies with pupil participation, even the less likely children should take part. They should be involved in the planning of such ceremonies or dramatic presentations and their opinions always treated seriously.

The guidance system has given rise, in some quarters, to a curiously wrong attitude on the part of teachers who are, officially, not yet involved in it. Teachers, class tutors though they may be designated, find the appointment of guidance teachers with responsibility payment a ready-made excuse for contracting out of extra voluntary services. They argue that, since the house guidance teachers' duties are concerned with the social lives of the pupils, they alone should be responsible for all the non-academic activities in the school — sport, clubs, stage shows, concerts, parties and so on. This is regrettable for the harmful effect it has on the spirit of the school which draws most of its strength from such activities.

And as for the counselling, every teacher should be, in some respects, a guidance teacher. Indeed the system will only work effectively if there is widespread liaison between the house staff and the others. Formally or informally, an exchange of information and opinions about problem pupils should be going on all the time. Guidance teachers should not be too touchy about non-guidance teachers transgressing on their ground. Likewise non-guidance teachers, when they find themselves advising the pupils about personal matters, should keep the house master informed. In this as in so much else, teamwork is all important.

Another function of the house master is to build up the morale of the house and of all its members by happy assemblies, vigorous and original activities, social functions involving members of the house and often their parents, making school life enjoyable and sometimes exciting, turning, one might say, the house into a home. Nor must he play down that part of his job which is concerned with the rehabilitation of the waifs and strays of his house. These present a challenge which will tax all his patience, his stamina, and his ability to control his temper and to suffer disappointments without succumbing to despair. His greatest temptation, in respect of the flotsam and jetsam of his house, will be to pass them over to the various experts and agencies which are available to help to deal with deprived or problem children. The advice of these qualified experts is usually helpful and should be made full use of, but that is quite a different matter from regarding these outside services as disposal bins. How relieved the teacher often is when the child departs to a psychiatric centre or a children's panel or an assessment centre. Indeed the notion of centres for delinquents is gaining in popularity among teachers but to have to find an answer to one's problems outside the school should not be a matter for satisfaction. One should rather take the view that if a pupil has to go elsewhere than the school for help it may well imply some shortcoming on the part of the school. It should be hoped that he would come back and, when he comes, let him be welcomed. A process is not a substitute for a home; and home is 'where they've got to take you in'. Yet there have been instances of teachers vigorously opposing readmission of problem children who have been removed temporarily for some reason or other. They have not perhaps heard of the greatest of New Testament stories, the Prodigal Son. If our school is a Christian community, we should be prepared to put up with a lot.

In many schools the guidance staff take responsibility for social education, a general term which loosely embraces a wide range of extra-curricular activities, timetabled within the school's working day, two or three periods or even a whole afternoon. The syllabus may include many arts and crafts not included in the normal curriculum, drama for stage presentation, choirs, singing and instrumentalists' groups, dancing, hobbies like philately, aeromodelling, numismatology; pastimes like bridge or chess or draughts, table-tennis, local history and archaeology, or social service outside the school like meals-on-wheels, nursery schooling; and, of course, a great variety of sports that may have an element of novelty, as judo, trampolining, orienteering and so on. The list of possibilities seems almost endless. The justification for this branch of social education is that it may provide an interesting and rewarding leisure-time activity which the pupil may carry on in adult life.

Usually the whole school is involved in this project at the same time and not only the guidance teachers but the whole staff have to take their share of the work. Regrettably their assistance is often given halfheartedly if not resentfully. Thus the opportunity these periods present to capture the interest and the enthusiasm of the substandard pupil is neglected. One cannot quite understand why there is such a lack of enthusiastic co-operation. The leisure activities add variety to the week. Relations between staff and pupils are more relaxed. They get to know one another. Academic competitiveness is absent and the atmosphere of these classes is not tarnished by frustration or a sense of failure. Teachers of the less colourful subjects might be expected to enjoy taking part in some creative craft or in a stage show with its own particular brand of excitement.

The obligation to take classes in this branch of the syllabus, education for leisure, reveals gaps in the professional assets of many teachers and in their sense of responsibility. With some the project is an invitation to indolence. With no examinations involved, such teachers are content to perform their duties at half-throttle, an approach that is reflected in the attitudes of their pupils, and boredom supervenes at every level. A misplaced and shallow legalistic interpretation of their role in the school produces the attitude that one should restrict oneself to the literal reading of contracts. 'I am employed as a teacher of Biology or French or Business Studies so why should I do someone else's work?' In other cases the poor showing some teachers make of taking classes in subjects other than their specialist professional ones, is due to a lack of versatility which is little short of incompetence. This type of education for leisure is a non-starter in many schools because some teachers seem to be unable to apply their general teaching techniques to one or other of their own leisure-time interests, whether it be chess or folk music, or archaeology, or amateur drama, or judo, or photography or local history, or golf, or philately, or aeromodelling or pottery, or flower arranging, or bookbinding, or metalwork, or gardening, or public speaking, or entomology, or bridge, or canoeing, or birdwatching or ESP investigation.

Since the situation I am describing will be found in almost all schools nowadays, it is time the colleges of education gave some attention to the problem of developing the competence of teachers in fields other than their specialist subjects. Since it is certain that the working hours of all will be substantially reduced in future years, it is a most serious failure in the education system if children pass out into adult life without hobbies or satisfying leisure-time interests, other than drinking, discoing, betting or playing the one-armed bandits.

The schemes of social or leisure-time education should make provision, and most of them do, for forming links with organisations outside the school, for studying the local environment and for exercises in charity with the aged or the handicapped or the disadvantaged nations. Industrial and commercial establishments are usually happy to co-operate with schools by welcoming visiting parties; the same applies to newspapers and centres of local administration. Organisers of this branch of social education should, preferably, be local people with many contacts in the area and what they plan should be closely related to the routine careers counselling in the school.

Social education as part of the school experience has a wider connotation than concern with leisure-time activities, hobbies or creative pursuits. It is generally taken to include the inculcation of standards of behaviour that would be considered desirable by the average parent or teacher. This branch of social education should be the concern not of the guidance teachers alone but of every teacher in the school. The spectrum ranges from the discouragement of personal habits likely to be physically or psychologically harmful to more public attitudes like good manners and responsible citizenship.

The habits of a large proportion of our adolescents do not support the view that we have been very successful in this sphere of education. How should we approach it?

A wide range of techniques are in use, with the emphasis on visual aids and classroom discussions.

Illustrated lessons, usually involving films, may be effective in demonstrating the dangers in certain personal habits such as alcoholism, smoking and drug addiction and also in sexual abuse. As for good citizenship, classroom discussions on simulated hypothetical situations are thought to be useful.

Discussions and debates, the modernists set great store by them. Certainly they are valuable in encouraging oral self-expression and, if properly conducted, an attitude of tolerance towards those who may disagree with one. These discussions are valuable too, for widening the children's horizons with respect to social and environmental issues on which many of them, as adults, will take a stand as, for example, nuclear weapons, environmental pollution, factory farming, fox-hunting, vivisection, the poverty of the Third World, euthanasia, the destruction of wildlife and so on. But when it comes down to day-to-day personal conduct and habits it is doubtful if the discussion method has ever had much effect.

Unless expertly conducted, classroom discussions seldom follow a clear-cut line, the progress of the debate being repeatedly hampered by irrelevancies and by the variety of personal expressions of opinion. Seldom does a conclusion emerge. Does anyone, adult or child, ever change his habitual behaviour as a result of a debate or a discussion? Modes of conduct are not settled by reason or logic but by the values one has come to accept.

When the immature participate in a debate, the decision finally arrived at is anyone's guess. A few years ago there was a catchword applied to school projects, debates and arguments. It was the word 'open-ended'. An open-ended discussion in a classroom was one in which the teacher was not supposed to influence the course of the debate or lead it to his own predetermined conclusion, otherwise he would be guilty of the unpardonable sin of injecting his own 'middle-class values' into the minds of working-class children and setting up traumatic psychological conflicts in the process. It follows, I think, that, if the teacher had a section of urban vandals, they might very well decide by a majority that telephone-booth-wrecking was a highly commendable pastime and the teacher would not be entitled to demur. So much for conducting social education by open-ended discussion!

With most children, the world inside the classroom is usually regarded as a place by itself with no particular relationship to the outside world. A classroom debate might very well decide that dropping litter is an objectionable habit but there will be no significant difference in the untidiness of the school tuckshop precincts during the following interval. The debate was a classroom experience; eating a lollipop at the tuckshop a part of one's real life — quite different.

How then is social education (acceptable behaviour) to be conducted? Here are four lines of approach.

These are: training in mannerly behaviour; setting examples of desirable conduct; commenting by praise and blame on real incidents that happen in the school; and placing as many pupils as possible in situations where they will be obliged to make a choice between alternative modes of conduct.

First training. It is an old-fashioned approach. There will be a school code of conduct presented to the pupils in the form of a set of rules that will specifically prohibit bullying, violence, vandalism, smoking, drinking, obscene language, all serious offences. However happy one would wish the school family to be, we must never forget that it is a community under law, a community which must protect the weak and vulnerable against those who would exploit their weakness and vulnerability for their own interests.

In this code of conduct a number of less serious offences, as, for example, breaches of good manners, will also be clearly defined. One of the most fatuous arguments put up recently by those who recommend a 'progressive' attitude to school discipline is that if you reduce the number of rules, you will have fewer infringements of rules. They refrain from noting that you will also have more of the mind of conduct that the rules were intended to prevent. If your purpose is to have good manners, what can be wrong with making them obligatory?

Prohibitions should include bawling in corridor and dining hall, jeering at fellow-pupils who find themselves in embarrassing situations, throwing down litter, refusing to queue when it is necessary, neglecting normal courtesies in dining hall or tuckshop ('please' and 'thank you'), disturbing staff conversations by noisy distractions and interruptions, failure to conduct a stranger unsure of his whereabouts, or to hold swing doors open for approaching teachers. And so on — every school will be able to add to the number of such injunctions appropriate to its own situation.

If such minor misdemeanours are mentioned in the official code of behaviour, it need not imply that the authorities are constantly on the lookout for trivial offences but merely that it provides a ready frame of reference when it is thought necessary to comment on behaviour in the school.

It must be remembered that many children, concerned about how they behave, like to have the guidelines exactly delineated; such will appreciate exact instructions about what is expected of them in day-to-day situations.

So much for the code of conduct. Let us now consider the importance of setting examples of civilised behaviour. From their earliest days children have been in the habit of imitating adults and there is no reason to suppose that they will cease to do so when they reach the secondary school. With this in mind every teacher will never forget that he is part of the pupils' school experience and that what he says and does should serve as a model for his pupils, the more so if he has a positive personality. I shall deal later with how the teacher's moral attitudes might influence his pupils in respect of his approach to his subject and his handling of classroom incidents. It is sufficient for the moment to say that ordinary good manners exhibited consistently by the staff and headmaster of a school are bound to 'rub off' on other members of the school community and if enough attention is paid to this, the school will become a more civilised place. If teachers consistently say 'good morning' to pupils in classroom and corridor, it won't be long before the children themselves anticipate the greeting. A demand for punctuality will be reinforced if the teacher himself is always in time. Most important is the fulfilling of engagements that have been freely contracted and the keeping of promises. How often are teachers themselves guilty of conduct which they would not accept from the pupils — shouting, interrupting a conversation and so on! It is dangerously simplistic to say that teachers should also behave naturally in their classrooms. The image they offer must be somewhat better than what is natural to them. A considerable amount of self-scrutiny will be advisable before they decide how far they are justified in being natural and how far they will be obliged to 'put on an act'.

The third way by which some progress might be made in improving children's behaviour is by immediate comment on real situations which happen in the school. This is quite a different matter from the discussion of hypothetical situations in a social education classroom period, or the role-playing beloved of speech/drama teachers. The comment will relate the real incident to the school's code of conduct and, at the same time, will imply a set of values accepted as absolutes. It will be made at school assembly or in the corridor or the classroom, directly to those involved and in the hearing of others. It will be effective only if the one who is commenting has obtained the respect of the pupils. The comment will take the form of praise or blame but must be seriously made, never jocularly, and yet with no element of righteous indignation. A teacher or head who loses control of himself, loses control of the situation. But respect is the prerequisite. The average pupil fears the censure and appreciates the praise of one whom he likes, respects or admires. The notion that bad behaviour is letting the teacher down is old fashioned but still valid.

And, just as scholars may behave acceptably just because they value the regard of those whom they respect, so we must feel in the same way about their school. If a school community sense has developed (and that is what this book is about), they will not need to be reminded that disgraceful conduct tarnishes the reputation of the school and honourable conduct enhances it. This is an argument for school uniform, the wearing of which is a constant reminder of what the school expects of its pupils.

The fourth way in which progress may be obtained in social/moral education is by putting as many of the pupils as possible into situations where they will have to ask themselves which is the good course of action, the right decision. This is an argument for creating the maximum number of posts of responsibilities where the notion of duty, reliability, public service and good manners will never be far from the pupil's mind. The office will make certain demands which must be clearly brought to the attention of its holder. It might be argued that the number of such positions in a school is strictly limited but this is not so. Once it becomes the policy of the school that the maximum number of such posts be found, they will be found: in classroom duties, playground and litter control, in the organisation of sport and many other school activities, as captains and secretaries of clubs and teams, hosts to welcome and conduct visitors, as messengers for promoted staff, and so on. The maximum initiative will be left to these pupils and staff interference will be usually limited to telling those concerned that they are doing well or ill.

To sustain ethical values in the school the assemblies are all important. There, praise and blame are dispensed, school happenings are evaluated in terms that emphasise their moral importance, congratulations are given publicly for acts of kindness, deeds of valour and other honourable performances.

Much that I have been saying about the promotion of good social values will apply equally to moral education and, indeed, exact differentiation between the two concepts is not easy. The word 'social' tends to connote adjustment to the interests of the society in which you find yourself; 'moral' implies the exhibiting of a virtue in a positive, personal way, making the right but more difficult choice. Teachers of certain subjects (English, History, Modern Studies, perhaps Art and Music) may, in the classroom, encounter the traditional concepts of Beauty, Goodness and Truth, a trio which almost sums up the educational aim of producing an all-round person. The great classics of literature display goodness in a setting of beauty and harmony. The works of Homer were a standard textbook for the moral training of Athenian children. The great allegories of our own literature — *The Pilgrim's Progress, Everyman, The Faerie Queen, The Dark Tower* by Louis McNeice, and, of course, the parables of the New Testament — present virtue in a setting of verbal beauty. Even in the sombre world of Shakespearean tragedy the dismal wastes of failure and suffering, where 'good things of day begin to droop and drowse' are illumined by acts of courage, loyalty and compassion. Unfortunately many modern teachers of English concentrate obsessively on the literature of abject surrender, of evil without redemption, of misery without hope. The will to resist the ravages of time and chance, and courage, 'the lovely virtue', and love, 'which moves the sun in heaven and the other stars', hardly rate a mention in their English syllabuses. One would think that some of them had been commissioned to effect the demoralisation of British youth. Are faith and hope 'played out'? Poetry used to be visionary, many splendoured. Now the cynics have it all their own way.

I write these things in the hope that some time, somewhere, a teacher of English might be emboldened to identify moral values in his studies of the great English writers.

Progress in social and moral education will depend on the general vitality of the school society. Some schools seems to have 'management' and not much else. The grey men wearily operate the levers that control the spiritless system. In a community of this kind there is not much sign of either good or bad for these terms relate only to action. Pupils must be involved in doing something more than merely sitting being instructed. Let them be organising happenings. Let them be participants in actions, functions, visiting the sick, welcoming the visitors, counselling new pupils, founding clubs, running their own newspapers, organising hobbies, managing school tuckshops and school bookshops, helping in the library, running cake-and-candy sales, providing posters and adverts, decorating their own common rooms, dealing with litter and graffiti — above all, taking initiatives.

As all this goes on and vital inter-personal relations develop, one would hope for the growth of a pervasive atmosphere of good will, an extension of pupils' friendships, an acceptance of new and binding obligations and a deepening of affection for the place where it is all happening — the school, their second home.

Chapter 9

The Teacher

It is time to consider the class teacher. What contribution does he make towards the pupil's school experience? How important is he? He will find the answer if he thinks of his class as a microcosm of the school community.

One cannot generalise for so much depends on individual personalities. The value of the contribution each teacher makes to the lifestyle of the school through the lifestyle of his pupils will depend on his commitment, his earnestness and his enthusiasm. These qualities are infectious. The best teachers are happy in their work. Their own schooldays were probably happy; they are at home in a school. They are glad to return after holidays and eager to resume friendships with colleagues and pupils. The crowded, turbulent world of school is their natural environment, the clattering and the clashing of the dining hall, the long corridors echoing to hundreds of footsteps, the sea of faces in assembly, strange and familiar, the cheerful clanging of bells, the freshly painted blackboards and the new pupils deceptively innocent looking in their new garments, this seems a good place to do one's work, always interesting, sometimes exciting, occasionally supremely rewarding. Whatever the disgruntled cynics of the profession may say, it is surely not an unforgiveable crime for the teacher to love his work and to love his school.

The spirit in which teachers approach their work is transmitted to the pupils. Many of the latter will respond favourably to the teacher who shows concern for their interests. Sincerity will not be misunderstood.

The spirit of the teacher will often be sharply tested. He may have to endure the derision of frustrated and disillusioned colleagues, or of unconcerned or censorious headmasters. It may be the teacher's lot to work in a depressed area among children pallid in visage, coarse in speech, churlish in manner, hostile to the society which seems to have offered them nothing. Yet a teacher of character will make the most of the hand he is dealt. He may have to shorten his horizons, harden himself to the acceptance of failure, draw on his every reserve of physical and mental stamina, of resourcefulness and versatility and of cold dogged determination not to give in.

Even with a class that is socially disagreeable, or even repellant, the mere passage of time seems to narrow the gap between teacher and pupils. The teacher's dedication in the most unpromising situation will outlast the pupils' hostility. Concern for their deprivation, humour in the face of their absurdities, appreciation of their insignificant talents and, above all, inexhaustible patience will turn the tide in his favour. Coming to terms with such intractable human material can be a notable experience, disturbing, exciting, strangely satisfying as, indeed it is so presented in that epic of teacher-pupil conflict 'To Sir, With Love'.

If the school climate is considered to be largely composed of personal relationships, one must question the doctrine of modern educationists that teaching should be replaced by 'learning situations'. Operating a projector or tape recorder, distributing and correcting worksheets, if these services compose the main battery of the teacher's resources, no wonder so many classrooms are featureless, colourless and boring. Nothing can be a substitute for a mature, well-stocked, animated human mind, capable of stimulating other minds, offering its abundant resources of knowledge, skill and imagination. When the teacher retreats into the shadows, the joy, the excitement, the eagerness which scholars used to know disappear with him. The clinical approach to classroom learning is based on the fallacy that education is a science—a process instead of a joyous adventure.

What the teacher has to contribute to the school experience of his pupils is, quite briefly, himself. The more complete a person he is the better for the children. From nine to four, he is 'on parade' and subject to inspection. He should, therefore, inspect himself from time to time and see whether he will pass muster. What he says and what he does in the various classroom situations are being continually observed, repeated, criticised, accepted, rejected, praised, condemned in playground, common room and in the homes of the children. His thoughtless off-the-cuff remarks may provoke amusement or scorn. His manner of speaking to his pupils may be deeply appreciated or make him an object of their hatred — hatred that smoulders in the mind of an offended one as long as life lasts. (Any reader who thinks this an exaggeration may find confirmation in his memories of his own schooldays.)

Every teacher is therefore projecting his values and his lifestyle on to the minds of his pupils. Not all of this influence will fade away with the passing years. To some of his pupils memories of his judgements may provide guidelines for their own conduct; the values that underlay what he said and did may help some to 'get their priorities right' when faced with moral options in their adult life. The teacher in the classroom is then, by his example, conducting moral and social education, whether he likes it or not. He is gravely at fault if he takes this responsibility lightly. It is vital.

The teacher is central to the classroom experience. Most of the things longest remembered by the pupils originate not from the 'hardware' of 'learning situations' but from the teacher's personal performance. His favourite jest, some unconsidered trifle light-heartedly thrown to his class, some rare moment when he divulged the profundity of his feelings about some social injustice or personal misfortune, some piece of clowning to lighten the texture of a tedious lesson, some gripping tale from his own early life, such fragments will often be recalled by former pupils as having an unaccountable significance in the body of scholastic matter that has survived the years. Very few teachers ever realise how potent a contribution they could make to their pupils' school experience by suspending their lesson for five minutes to recount an incident from their own life to illustrate an item in the lesson. Do the colleges of education ever demonstrate to students how they should speak to children, tell stories to them, 'hold them with the glittering eye' that portends wonder and mystery? Humour and imagination are invaluable adjuncts to teaching, though this may not occur to those who see no further than distributing the worksheets and correcting the scripts.

But every method has its pitfalls and one must pass a word of caution to the enthusiastic, extrovert teacher. He cannot say with certainty which of the statements he makes in class will be remembered and which will not. The ill-considered, indiscreet remark is just as likely, perhaps more likely, to be remembered by his pupils as the accurate, judicious one. Let him keep in mind that much that he says is going to be repeated in the children's homes, probably imprecisely. Some of the pupils are sensitive to political or religious nuances. These are dangerous quicksands.

I have argued that the classroom discussion is not the best medium for moral or social education but, nevertheless, the hundreds of judgements the teacher makes daily imply a code of values. The teacher must be consistent in the emphasis he puts on various forms of good and bad conduct and the pupils should not be in doubt as to what is acceptable and what is not. A virtue difficult to transmit to children nowadays is respect for the truth. Every hour of the day in every school in the country someone is telling a lie. Truth seems to be an obsolete conception. Dishonesty is normal in the worlds of politics and of advertising, in the pronouncements of celebrated public men, in the press, in commerce and, of course, in private life.

And automatic, quite shameless lying is normal amongst school pupils if there is the slightest whiff of danger to themselves or to their friends in any situation. If lies could bring down the lightning, to borrow a thought from Brandane's play, *Rory Aforesaid*, every school in the country would be dust and rubble. Pupils being interviewed about any delinquency will either completely deny responsibility for, or knowledge of, the happening or tell only part of the truth or deliberately confuse the investigation by irrelevance. What is most disturbing is that the liar is brazen, unashamed, often expert in the use of the 'deadpan' countenance acquired from watching crime investigations on TV, a technique unknown to pupils twenty-five years ago.

It is one thing to tell a lie, white, grey or black, and to feel somewhat less of oneself for having told it; but to be so lacking in self-respect that one habitually lies to advance one's own interests or to evade the consequences of irresponsibility and feels no conscientious scruples about having done so, that is surely the most depraved form of lying. A world where you cannot believe a word of what your fellows tell you has abandoned one of the contracts on which the stability of society depends.

Honesty then should be a top priority in teacher-pupil relationships. Without it one cannot have mutual confidence. If a teacher cannot trust his own pupils the flow of his personal influence on them is curtailed and soured. His happiness in the classroom is gone; his teaching becomes lifeless and mechanical — just a job of work.

Lying is inferior human conduct. If you doubt this, consider what you feel about a golf opponent who lies about the number of strokes he took in a bunker. One lie can poison or destroy friendships. The teacher will, therefore, not tell lies to his pupils and his pupils will not tell lies to him. Falsehood, in whatever from it occurs, will be exposed and punished.

A second quality that the teacher must display to his pupils as part of the school experience and of moral education is justice. The class teacher has a unique opportunity to display this quality in operation. Even with the best teachers, acts of delinquency will take place which, if repeated, may jeopardise the good order necessary for successful teaching. The teacher will have to judge the seriousness of such incidents and dispose of them by reprimand or punishment. He must be very careful. Nothing alienates a class more surely than inconsistency in applying the rules, unmistakeable favouritism, social discrimination or vindictiveness. The teacher should keep his class informed as to the principles behind his disciplinary policy and the reasons for his decisions. These explanations, provided that they are rational and fair, will increase the respect in which the teacher is held and the confidence the pupils have in him.

In particular the teacher must guard against favouritism. Few are immune from this weakness. It is inevitable that one should like one pupil more than another. When this occurs, it is not easily disguised. The tone of voice in which certain pupils are addressed, the frequency with which a pupil's christian name is used, the selection of certain pupils to run errands, inconsistency in imposing punishments, any or all of these may indicate the teacher's predilections and prejudices. The trend must be resisted. Perhaps the most effective answer to the temptation is to show a little extra favour to the pupil whom one does not like. Choose him for errands, drop a kind word now and then. This is a wise attitude for it is almost certain that, if you dislike a pupil, several of his other teachers will be reacting to him in a similar way and an Ishmaelite will be in process of creation. If all teachers adopted this attitude to the disagreeable personalities, some, at least, of the school delinquents might refrain from becoming leaders in the alternative society.

Truth in the classroom — justice in the classroom — what next? Perhaps it is respect for the precincts of the child's personality and his private life. Many who make profiles and many sociologist researchers, who intrude into our schools to get data for university and college theses, know nothing of this aspect. They tear the inner being of the child inside out for data about his parents and their relations with the child, his own feeling about authority, about sex, about his emotions and impulses and anxieties, about his attitudes to his teachers, about his loves and his terrors, his dreams and wild imaginings, about his vices and crimes and harmful habits.

This is what one is capable of doing if one has accepted the assumption that education is a science.

A teacher should keep himself clear of this enormity.

Let the teacher refrain from references to a child's parents (they may be divorced or one may be dead); remarks about the child's physical appearance or general references to handicapped children if there is one in the class; allusions to a pupil's love affair should he know of it; wounding sarcasm; words that belittle a pupil's mental capacity; allusions to any knowledge about the pupil's history that might embarrass him (a previous suspension from school for example); references to other members of the pupil's family; and, of course, jesting about any matter in respect of which the pupil might feel sensitive. An English teacher, for example, should not read a pupil's essay out to the class without that pupil's permission.

The pupil then should feel safe from intrusion by the teacher into his own inner kingdom. He should be free, too, from verbal assault. One of the first things a teacher has to attend to is the tone of his own voice. With tape recorders in general use, there is no excuse for his not doing so. Do children deserve, helpless, captive audience that they are, to be hectored, bullied, shouted at, shrieked at from morn to night? One can hear various forms of the aggressive voice in any school corridor; the strident voice that betokens a lady at the end of her patience; the heavily sarcastic shaft designed to penetrate all defences; the deep massive bombardment which makes a response unthinkable. A teacher who abandons such traditional styles of address and adopts a civilised man-to-man tone, such as educated people use to one another, will see his pupils look up at him with expressions of amazement and relief.

The teacher, as he enters, must make a good beginning — the appropriate salutation, 'Good morning' or 'Good afternoon' — and the class must respond. He must be scrupulous in thanking anyone who contributes anything useful to the procedures of the classroom, whether it is cleaning a blackboard, distributing equipment or offering to take part in a play. If the teacher arrives late he must apologise as, indeed, he must do if he makes an error in his teaching.

The teacher must see that every visitor to his classroom, whether he be the headmaster or a first year pupil, is treated with courtesy. Coarse manners must be outlawed — jeering at fellow-pupils who are in some kind of embarrassing position; proposing shy, inoffensive children for duties only to deride them; responding to items, humorously slanted, with raucous 'horse laughter'.

The attitude of the teacher to the taught must be one of friendly encouragement, particularly in the case of the less well endowed. Pupils must be sure that when they answer in class their efforts will not be ridiculed, either by teacher or fellow-pupil.

One of the most important principles that should be presented to pupils by their teacher (and exemplified in his own conduct) is the habit of keeping one's promise. It would make a pertinent school motto: My word is my bond. The idea is quite foreign to most of them and is frequently absent from any home training they may receive. Indeed, time and again, parents cause children, for some quite trivial reasons, to absent themselves from school functions they have promised to attend, rehearsals, sports practices etc. The required lesson may be driven home when pupils are engaged in school activities in respect of which they are required to be in a certain place at a certain time to do a certain job. There should be as many of such duties as possible. The briefing should emphasise how one's fellow-workers or team-mates are inconvenienced or 'let down' by the absence of one of the group. Similarly the notion of loyalty to, and continued membership of any group one has joined should be stressed to all members. The concept of obligation is the basis of every ethical code. Robert Frost made it memorable:

> 'I have promises to keep
> And miles to go before I sleep'.

Every teacher must solve for himself the problem of establishing good pupil-teacher relationships for the situation varies with the person concerned. A teacher has often to adopt a slightly different persona for each section that enters his room.

Sometimes pupil-teacher relations may be said to have reached vanishing point. With certain classes, disorderly elements may be in the ascendant and the teacher's efforts to turn his room into a centre of civilised behaviour are thwarted by those whose aim is to turn it into a bear garden. This nightmare is familiar to many young teachers. The clamour is vociferous, worse than it would be if no teacher were present; the boys are bawling to companions at the other side of the classroom; the girls chatter incessantly, everyone talking, nobody listening; the teacher is, in the main, ignored. What has happened in such cases is that pupil-pupil relations are dominant and pupil-teacher relationships have almost ceased to function. If the teacher should attempt to re-establish the latter by taking a pupil aside for an individual rebuke, the pupil will avoid looking at the teacher but will turn sideways, maddeningly, to grin to a friend some distance away. The friend may even come forward, uninvited, to give the other pupil some moral support. The whole class may join in the argument.

Desperate diseases require desperate remedies and the answer to this, not uncommon, situation is to demonstrate to the class that their behaviour is an offence to the whole school. A group of experienced teachers should meet in the room concerned and have a conference on the crisis, pinpointing the source of the trouble and discussing necessary action. This conference will take place in the presence and in the hearing of the whole class. For a class to have to sit and listen to an objective analysis of their group delinquencies will open their eyes to the importance of the episode and raise it to an unexpected level of seriousness. They will see their conduct measured against the ethic of the school for which (if the head has been doing his job properly) they will have some respect, and the detached, dispassionate manner in which the group of teachers discuss the case will throw into high relief the gravity of their offence. But even if the immediate trouble is dealt with, the teacher will not easily recover his lost authority and prestige. He will clearly have a lot to learn about the creation of a stable teacher-pupil relationship. Some teachers complete their careers without ever considering the quality of their relationship with their classes. I am not sure that the colleges of education see it as a problem. It is not to be achieved by a formula. The teacher has to feel his way towards it, trusting his instinct. What, in fact, he has to do is, at the beginning of his service in a school, to clothe himself in a somewhat bogus persona and then gradually remove it by almost imperceptible steps, until he can be his natural self in most of his classes. It is a delicate operation.

A teacher's relationship with his class is a growing, developing process. It is a dangerous mistake to reveal one's complete personality in the early days. If the teacher is something of a humorist, it is fatal. The pupils assume that they can take all sorts of liberties with such an agreeable fellow and in no time the class is beyond the teacher's control. Pupils inclined to disorder will be less dangerous in these early days if they are kept in the dark about the nature and strength of their enemy's resources. An inexperienced teacher with a new class should, by studied reticence, keep his pupils guessing as long as possible about his real nature and his likely reactions to classroom situations. It is a true adage that in the skirmishes of life as well as its battles, advantage will lie with the side that has most reserves, preferably in concealment, to call upon. And so during that period of mutual discovery, the teacher will control the revelation of his full personality or conceal its real nature by adoption of a persona more reticent than his own. But through time the contrived personality imperceptibly fades and there emerges a relaxed lifestyle in which the teacher, growing in confidence, can display the full range of his personal qualities. But not all teachers are sufficiently sensitive to the class atmosphere to recognise the time when they can relax and be their normal selves. Some teachers never get to the point when they can shed the false persona, the feigned image, and they retain it all their teaching lives. It may take many forms: sometimes it manifests itself as a cloak of infallibility; sometimes in a chilly, perpetually suspicious reserve; sometimes as a continuous flow of platitudinous cant; usually as a voice, hectoring, blustering, roaring, or in the case of the ladies, screeching, rasping, edgy with menaces (as if their eternal vociferation were not punishment enough).

When the young teacher has reached the point where he can relax in his classroom and speak and behave naturally, he may be said to have arrived. He must, however, take care that it is his best personality which is on display. The children deserve nothing less. (We all have a multitude of personalities, not all equally reputable.) This then will be the point of the teacher's maximum influence in his classroom. Without any apprehension of the pupils' derision or of an outbreak of disorder, the teacher will now be able freely to convey to their immature minds the wisdom of his mature years. Is this not what education is about — the old passing on to the young what they have learned about life? Nowadays the teacher is mainly an organiser of 'learning situations'; he has to conceal from his pupils what he knows; no knowledge is thought to be acceptable unless the pupil has found it for himself. The result in many cases (teaching projects for example) is that the pupil gathers a random harvest of fragmentary knowledge and is ignorant of a thousand things that the teacher could very well have told him had he not been inhibited by the postulates of the doctrine of pupil-centred education.

There is little vitality in an educational process unless in it mind meets mind. If you depersonalise it by removing the teacher's mind from what should be a reciprocal relationship and substituting a pupil-machine relationship, you impoverish the soil in which living ideas should grow. You will not improve your garden by putting your gardener on short time.

No. Let knowledge and wisdom flow luminously from the teacher's mind to that of the child. Let the teacher occasionally digress from his lesson to quote something apposite from his own experience: the mistakes he himself has made, the pitfalls, as he has known them, to be avoided, vital decisions that led to success or failure in his own life, his inner struggles and the people who influenced him. Nor will there be harm if sometimes what he tells them is illuminated by a vision of the good life, of the virtues, of the experiences that make for contentment and of memories that have retained some element of inspiration over the years. Let him sometimes speak of his own family life, of his parents and the training they gave him and of the good and the evil he has encountered in his teaching career and the pupils, saints and reprobates he has known. Provided these digressions are not over-frequent, he will be listened to with rapt attention, for real episodes from one's life usually make a more direct impact than the remote things in books. A teacher who has a flair for animated digressions will vivify his narratives with old proverbs and rhymes, with local allusions, with portraits of remembered personalities, with legends and traditions and descriptions of places far away. Thus will he blazon the lessons in his syllabus with the colourings of real life, the teacher's own real life. If his teaching is remembered in the future by some of his pupils, it will be because he has given them himself along with the lesson, the memorable moment when he closed the book and said, 'Listen and I will tell you what once happened to me'.

Sadly the manner in which many teachers talk to their classes leaves much to be desired. No matter his subject, his own classroom converse should be a model for the children. The tone should be friendly, ideas should be lucidly arranged, narration should be graphic, enunciation should be clear and audible, gestures should be vivid and the whole dissertation never prolonged to the extent of boredom. His influence for good will flow through his easy, conversational, relaxed and friendly discourse.

There is danger in making classroom teaching a clinical exercise. If we are thinking of producing complete men and women the emotions should be properly stimulated by elements in the lessons. A good teacher will at times evoke wonder, curiosity, compassion, indignation, affection — but all in moderation. The digressions I have been referring to — the reminiscences and the anecdotes — should be reserved for well-chosen occasions, the end of the day or Friday afternoon. Such digressions will be a welcome relief from the interminable copying of material from books, which seems to be an indispensable concomitant of the project method or the sheaves of individual worksheets which descended, 'thick as autumnal leaves', on the pupils' desks when the egalitarian theorists made the discovery that all pupils in comprehensive schools were not of equal ability.

Most of us have seen a picture 'The Boyhood of Raleigh' with an old sailor telling two boys of his adventures overseas and pointing out towards the Spanish Main. This, I think, was emotional education and there is a place for it. Interwoven with the material of the syllabus of any subject there may be threads of enchantment, romance, adventure, humour. Wonder can be evoked, curiosity stimulated, doors thrown open in the imagination. If the teacher has access to that kind of magic (and not all have) it may kindle something that is tragically absent from modern classrooms and that is enthusiasm. More of this shortly.

The case I have been arguing for greater teacher participation in the teacher-pupil relationship implies that he will speak more to his class than has been customary with modern methods. This implies greater responsibility as regards the subjects discussed and the language used. Some of what he says is going to be remembered by some of his audience, possibly for years, possibly for a lifetime. It may be quoted by pupils to their fellows in the playground and to their families at home, to interested, amused, astonished or deeply shocked parents. And, a more disturbing thought, there may be ascribed to him remarks that he did not make at all; he will frequently be misreported without having the chance to put the record straight.

The friendly, relaxed manner, the conversational style of address, the civilised tone — all these are desirable and should be normal. And one hopes these would become models for the pupils' style of conversation. But again there are dangers. An easy-going, intimate style may be a cloak for indolence and casualness in the routines of the classroom, a haphazard approach which loses sight of goals, all leading to the final disintegration of the class as a working unit. This can come about in most classes if the teacher lacks that all-essential entity which it is his first and foremost duty to bring to his class.

And that thing is will.

Will is a driving force coming from somewhere in the human mind and directed on all factors in a situation so that they will be assembled and mobilised with an end in view. It involves determination to surmount difficulties and discipline to ensure that the fullest use is made of all faculties and powers and assets, discipline imposed either from within or without.

Yet the modern teacher has been so much brainwashed by theories of liberty that he is almost ashamed to use the word 'discipline'. One would think that no longer was there any need for it in our modern world. Are we then well on our way to producing ballet without discipline, orchestral pieces without discipline, actors without discipline, astronauts without discipline, gymnasts without discipline, firemen without discipline, armies without discipline?

There are few achievements of any worth in the world without discipline — and that means the will driving people on to do things which, without the will, they would reject as being disagreeable to them. And so in the classroom there must sometimes be this driving force, either coming from the pupils themselves, because they wish to progress, or more probably, from the teacher.

Closely associated with discipline is authority, a word similarly unpopular nowadays. No matter how liberal the teacher's regime may be, there will be occasions when arguing, cajoling, pleading, suggesting, persuading will be inappropriate ways of getting something done and an order, rapped out sharply, will be the proper initiation of action. The pupils should recognise the tone and leap to attention and obedience. They must be conditioned to respond to the peremptory tone the moment it is used. If a fire breaks out in the school and the pupils are moving in the wrong direction and the teacher shouts an order to redirect them, there must be an instant reaction to that order. But if the voice is that of one whose authority they are in the habit of ignoring, then the stampede in the wrong direction will go on, perhaps with disastrous consequences. It is folly to argue that authority can be eliminated from school relationships. Conditions for quiet study in class depend on the teacher having authority. A theatrical performance may be ruined because the teacher in charge of off-stage crowds cannot keep performers quiet. Accidents may happen at bus queues because the pupils regard the master in charge as one 'whom nobody bothers about'. Teachers who never acquire the authoritative tone are failing in their duty to the parents who expect that their children will be protected from danger when they commit them to the care of teachers.

In every subject there are branches that are uninteresting or unattractive because of their difficulty but which are, at the same time, indispensable for the full understanding of the subject. There may be basic formulae and definitions to be committed to memory, a process to which the modern boy and girl are markedly averse.

There will be occasions therefore when the teacher will have to drive his pupils and to drive himself — and incidentally teach a moral lesson when he is doing it. An object lesson in determination, a demonstration of will in action, these are valuable elements in the school experience which, if remembered, may make all the difference between triumph and disaster in later life. The will of the teacher that his teaching should be successful does not mean the imposition of a severe discipline. The teacher's will emerges as briskness, alertness, purposefulness, instant encouragement and instant reproof and continuing concern about standards. He aims at a climate of serious attentiveness in his classroom. He will be well prepared for his lesson before the class appears, will start promptly, define his objective, attain it, revise, recapitulate all that has been taught or learned in the period. His pupils will depart, aware that the period has not been wasted and the teacher will have retained their respect and confidence.

Closely associated with 'will' and 'discipline' is the enthusiasm or spirit evinced by the teacher who has a real love of his subject. It does not follow that this approach will be fully reciprocated by his pupils but, usually, the standard of attentiveness is increased if the teacher is throwing himself, heart and soul, into the lesson.

Admittedly there has never been a time when enthusiasm and vision seemed more irrelevant to the teacher-pupil relationship than the present. One sees one's former pupils, all self-respect abandoned, loitering aimlessly in streets adjoining the school, their vitality long since crushed in the wasteland of unemployment. The sensitive teacher will be haunted by the awareness of his own dishonesty in ever having suggested that his subject was a useful preparation for a career. This is the nature of the malaise which is darkening the atmosphere of many schools.

But 'when the worst comes, the worst is going'. The teacher must have faith to 'do the best of things in the worst of times', and must hold fast to the belief that to study something is always better than not to study anything; that thorough teaching, geared to a pupil's intellectual level, may leave in his mind something of ultimate value; and that through the medium of the subject some awareness of intellectual, cultural and moral values may emerge. By faith, rather than by certainty, the teacher may save from extinction the flame of ardour in which he entered his first classroom one bright morning long ago.

No matter what changes take place in the curriculum there will always be lower stream pupils. There is an ever-present danger that the teacher will adopt an entirely mistaken attitude to these. Since the habitual delinquents and the 'work-shy' are all to be found in this group, teachers often generalise about the whole group and dismiss them all as scholastically negative and socially non-co-operative. But there are usually dozens of inconspicuous, quiet ones, not clever but yearning to be taught something, to make some slight academic progress. Yet how often the processes that go on in their classrooms imply not progress but 'passing the time'. The pupils know quite well the value of the fare that is being provided for them and with a helpless shrug, concealing a despondent heart, slip into the lassitude which has become the prevailing mood of their school experience.

But the teacher should take thought and bestir himself. The axiom for teaching at every level is that the class must leave the classroom at the end of the lesson aware that in that period they have acquired new knowledge, or new understanding or new skill. And this applies even when the prospects do not exceeed the possibility of minimal progress. No matter how slow the progress, pupil and teacher must set out on the journey into new areas of knowledge and understanding, in brotherly company.

> 'Page and master forth they set,
> Forth they set together,
> Through the rude wind's wild lament
> And the bitter weather.'

Even if the academic partnership seems to verge on futility, there must be a moral relationship of greater significance. The teacher must make it clear that he values these pupils, if not as scholars, certainly as human beings for their good behaviour, their efforts, and their co-operativeness. If there is anything in the subject at all that they can do successfully, let it be acknowledged and praised. The morale of such a section may well be saved if the teacher can initiate a project which consists of preparation for some future event. The pupils are sharers in an enterprise, partners in a team moving forward to an intriguing adventure. The future event may be an exhibition, a musical or dramatic show, an educational visit, a gym or dancing display or a mannequin parade or the making of a film or a sound programme with tape recorders. Whether all the members can be motivated to play a part in such projects will depend, however, very largely on the composite character of the class.

The crucial factor in pupil/teacher relationships is the composite character of the class — here is the whole nub of class management and a teacher who does not know about this curious phenomenon will not get very far. The communal character is in some respects an amalgam of all the personalities in the section but it invariably reveals a bias originating from the two or three most positive personalities. An observant teacher of first year will not fail to notice a communal spirit emerging and crystallising during the first two months. Once it has hardened, usually about Christmas, nothing will dissolve it. Individuals, previously regarded as of neutral personality, take on the prevailing colouring of the unit. And so it comes about that one class begins to be regarded as attentive, another restless, another high-spirited, another humourless, another responsible, another cynical, another docile, another refractory, another industrious, and so on.

Sometimes the source of the prevailing mood of the class is covert; occasionally a person with a gift for leadership, honourable or depraved, openly takes charge of the class and dictates the policy. The source of the communal spirit may be a group of children who have been promoted from the same primary school.

Now if the class spirit or communal character is of a kind antipathetic to the ethos of the school, or to the benign climate which is being developed in the school at large, then its presence must be a matter for concern. Early detection is of paramount importance. The danger must be brought out into the open. The various teachers of each newly formed section should consult one another a few weeks after the beginning of term and agree about some kind of joint action if a remedy is required. If a cynical, aggressive or non-co-operative trend is discernible, the origin of it must be identified and the influence of the keymen neutralised. Once more it will be found to be sound policy to take the whole class into the teacher's confidence. The mischievous element at large in the section must be openly described to the class and the prestige of the saboteurs deflated. Extreme measures, you may think. But I have known a disruptive or malicious attitude, emanating from one person, contaminate irretrievably a section of thirty pupils. Almost any expedient, even the removal of a pupil to another class, would have been justifiable in trying to reverse the drift towards anarchy originating from the activities of one individual.

Such a remedy, if unavoidable, is nevertheless negative. The class teachers should combine in strengthening the co-operative elements in the class, encouraging them to maintain their responsible and respectable attitudes in the face of contrary currents. And those who are delicately poised between the two conflicting relationships should be won over to the good side by assigning to them duties which will involve them in constructive service. As for the leaders, one must not give up hope.

The kind of contribution which the classroom teacher may make to the experience of his pupils will depend to some extent on whether or not he has a sense of humour.

A sense of humour is, in some circumstances, an instrument of class control. A reproof for minor misconduct contained in a lighthearted comment suggests to the delinquent that the teacher's concern for conduct is really part of an essentially friendly attitude. There is no need to indulge in an outburst of righteous indignation every time a pupil drops a pencil. One should keep one's thunder for the major delinquencies.

The conscious injection of humour into teaching methods is surprisingly effective. It provides a pleasurable context for the lesson; it reveals an engaging human trait in the personality of the teacher which colours the subject he is expounding, in an attractive way; and it has a retentive value, the lesson being remembered along with the joke that accompanied it. Ask any adult what he has retained of school subjects in his memory and, as like as not, he will tell of some amusing situation or remark that is associated in his mind with the lesson.

Sometimes the humorous remark comes from the class and not from the teacher. The teacher then has to make a split-second decision. Is the intervention to be classified as 'cheek' and merit an icy response? Should he join in the laughter? Nine times out of ten the latter reaction is more prudent. It depends on the spirit in which the remark was made. If the remark was really funny, a pompous 'we are not amused' reaction by the teacher will definitely leave him at a disadvantage.

But many jokes in our depraved society raise issues which are moral rather than social. Cruel humour, sick humour, these are forms that are typical of a society becoming increasingly callous. Jokes about illness, about death, about the suffering of animals can only coarsen the minds of those who listen to them or who tell them. If the ethos of the school is Christian and embraces compassion towards the suffering, whether of man or animal, the unchristian implications of this type of humour should not be ignored.

Fashions in humour change and these changes may throw light on the nature of our society. It is instructive and not altogether encouraging to note the type of incident that evokes laughter in the fourteen- and fifteen-year-old pupils in our secondary schools.

The only occasions on which many of them laugh is when they are jeering at the discomfiture of a fellow-pupil. An instance would be when a teacher selects a pupil to take an unusual part in a lesson (acting as a model in the art class, taking part in a play). Harmless fun it may be but it is not an acceptable habit to acquire — to mock at the embarrassment of others. Apart from being unmannerly, it is harmful to the atmosphere of the class for it discourages participation in, for example, new experimental work. The teacher's position, as a source of all classroom business, is seriously threatened when the pupils begin to pay more attention to their classmates than they do to him.

Another form of classroom humour, even more distasteful, is the double entendre, a technique acquired by some of the more depraved pupils from the sexually obsessed comedians on the media. This squalid element can vitiate the serious content of any lesson. Once a pupil, predisposed to that type of humour, has got hold of the idea the game can be played ad infinitum in any classroom in any subject. The joker concentrates on every word the teacher uses and as soon as he detects one that could bear an indecent connotation, he turns towards his class-mates with a meaningful smirk. Familiarly known to his fellows as an instigator of this type of diversion, he knows that the faint shadow of a smile may be sufficient to direct the attention of the class to the indecent allusion. No one who has any respect for the subject he is teaching will tolerate this wanton interference with his presentation. Sweet reasonableness is not the answer to such conduct.

To be taught by a good teacher can be an impressive experience. The rapport between him and his class is all embracing, mercurial, vibrating through a multitude of points of contact. The best teacher reacts like lightning to a thousand situations each day. He knows the name of each pupil and has a specific relationship with each. A word of praise or encouragement here, a word of reproof or warning there, a prompt piece of advice to an individual, a sharp adjuration to the whole class, a swift assertion of authority at a first sign of potential disorder, a brief demonstration of the right way to do something, an occasional joke or an apposite anecdote, an enquiry about someone's health, a direction about homework, all these blended with drive, confidence, imagination, humour, all these compose the classroom experience.

Pupils who have sat at the feet of such exponents of the art of teaching will garner a harvest of memories which will probably constitute the main body of their education so far as it is a continuing influence in their lives.

The teacher's main concern should be the atmosphere of his class-room. It is a matter of achieving a balance between opposites: between work and relaxation; between the serious and the lighthearted; between privilege and duty; between oral and written work; between teaching and questioning; between commands and consultation; between democracy and dictatorship. To lean too heavily towards one or other of these pairs of opposites may induce boredom or inattention and turn the class work into predictable routine, lacking variety, surprise and vitality.

The teacher should take the widest possible interest in the school activities of his pupils. He should attend the school concert, the football final, the inter-house quiz, the dancing display. His presence at such events emphasises that they are important and the pupils are very anxious to know what their teachers thought of the performance and gratified to hear words of praise or congratulation. They will experience feelings of pride and loyalty at such moments and an affection for the school for which they are doing their best.

Although a teacher's room is his island kingdom, he should not feel himself marooned in it. If he needs advice or moral support, he should be able to obtain these from colleagues conveniently located and prepared to co-operate. An effective method of putting an idea over to pupils is for several of the staff to discuss it in the hearing of the pupils. What is being said gathers weight when pupils learn that it is a matter of serious concern to their teachers. What is overheard will become the subject of playground conversation and if the teachers are well liked, their quoted remarks will have influence on popular opinion. The teacher's image will benefit when he is heard speaking in relaxed, non-classroom tones. Pupils knowing that they are being encouraged to listen to a teachers' conversation will be agreeably impressed and even flattered by the trust implied.

One of the merits of open-plan school architecture is that this practice of public inter-staff conversations becomes common. The procedure has a telling effect on the maintenance of discipline. The open discussion of a behavioural problem or incident, by several teachers in the hearing of the delinquent and his classmates, makes an impact twice as forcible as if only one teacher were involved.

Inter-teacher liaison and co-operation are much more easily achieved in schools where it is the practice for the whole staff to assemble in a common room at intervals.

The provision of subject bases in the new secondary schools, while administratively useful, has encouraged a feeling of departmental separation which is bad for the community spirit. Departments withdraw into their shells and do not know, let alone participate in, the activities and the projects of other departments. The Modern Language people do not know that the Homecraft Department are running a mannequin parade; the English Department are ignorant of the Gym Department's dancing display; the History Department do not know that the Drama classes are rehearsing *A Man For All Seasons*. If there is to be a kind of dynamism in the onward march of a school (and the metaphor of any army advancing is not too far-fetched) then everyone should know what everyone else is contributing to the success of the campaign and this will not happen if each department isolates itself in a remote subject base.

But in a staff common room one should feel the whirring dynamos. The cheerful ebb and flow of conversation there makes the individual teacher aware of his participation in a great enterprise.

On these daily occasions a teacher may begin to feel more closely identified with the fortunes of the school, more closely related to its developing history, the dazzling complexity and richness of its life.

Chapter 10

The Pupils

If the climate of a school consists of the sum total of inter-personal relationships and personal influences, then the contribution of the thousand-plus pupils to that process is, arguably, as important as the influence of their eighty teachers. This is something that seems never to occur to the pupils; they assume that all the initiatives lie with the head and his staff. That may be true of the corporate life of the school but one must not discount the effects that strong personalities among pupils have on others. We have seen how the composite character of one class may be formed by the dominant influence of a few pupils; even so the customs, attitudes and habits that prevail among the seniors may be based on the behaviour of a few 'leading lights'.

A school that is serious about social education must persuade all the pupils that each has a contribution to make to the lifestyle of the school by setting the right kind of example, especially to the younger children. The further up the school one finds oneself the greater is the responsibility to conform to the model of the good school citizen. How does this happen?

A good start to a secondary school career should be the notion that education is a voyage of exploration, a period of discovering the interior of one's own being, one's hidden talents and hitherto unrealised potential. The school is a practice ground where one tries oneself out and one ought to make the most of the many avenues to be explored in the search for one's own special talent. The mainspring of a school career should be continuous curiosity about the avenues along which one ventures in search of a hidden part of oneself.

Of course all the avenues are not equally inviting or properly signposted. There are subjects seemingly too difficult for the average person and teachers who can neither explain nor inspire. Some subjects, therefore, will prove to be blind alleys for some individuals and the problem then is to maintain morale in the face of disappointment and failure.

It is the test of the quality of the school as a community that the failure of a pupil in individual subjects should not lead to school

rejection. The school should be offering to all its pupils the widest possible spectrum of enriching experiences, cultural, intellectual, aesthetic,
recreational, social and spiritual, some of which stimulate interest and
uncover hidden talents. The reality, however, is rather different.

Pupils enter the secondary school with confidence that a new,
exciting world is opening out before them. They feel that life is worth
living in a place that seems to be offering them so much. The
experience of most of them for the next two or three years is progressive disenchantment. Their initial anticipation of a wonderfully
exciting school career is seldom fulfilled. A proportion of them join the
ranks of the alternative society and develop habits of indolence and
misbehaviour. They soon drift away from extra-curricular activities in
which they were originally interested; they abandon the school
uniform; they have neither interest nor pride in anything that happens
inside the school. Real life for them is what they can experience in the
evenings or at weekends; the TV, the videos, the disco, pop records,
football spectating, later alcohol. The school means nothing.

The new courses and the additions to the curriculum about to be
introduced in Scotland are intended to ensure that all pupils will work
at levels where they can progress. If hopes are fulfilled it will be easier
than it has been to build a healthy pupil/school relationship.

But even as things are, it is possible to have a school community
which can offer an experience of value to every citizen, where morale
is high and where the pupils, even those moderately endowed, will not
feel, as many do now, that their education has been a futile exercise.

We shall come closer to closing or, at least, to narrowing the gap
between the two worlds in the school if we think of it as a family and
try to persuade the children to feel and act as if it were. In a good family
every member is important and everything that a member does or
experiences or suffers is considered to be important by every other
member of the family. In a good family there is affection, a caring
attitude to one another. A weak member of the family, physically or
mentally, automatically gets more affection and care: he or she is not
discarded or turned out of the home. In a good family everyone is
interested in the lives, the affairs, the exploits, the successes and failures
of the others. Triumph and disaster are shared experiences. They may
bicker among themselves but when the crunch comes they stand
together. They take some pride in their history and traditions and try
not to let one another down by incurring some disgrace. 'We were
entrusted to one another,' says Elizabeth Bowen, 'in the days that
mattered.'

There must be guidance given to the children, in their early days in the school, as to how they should treat one another. In some continental schools you will see children shaking hands with one another in the morning in the playground.

The staff should greet them courteously and they should reciprocate. The prevailing mood should be gracious.

The pupils should learn how ill mannered it is to scoff at anyone who is in an embarrassing situation. Or to take advantage of new, young, inexperienced teachers. These are members of the family and should be assisted and sustained.

It should be understood that every pupil ought to participate in at least one extra-curricular activity. Once a pupil has joined he should be given some duty connected with it so that he may develop a sense of responsibility.

Playing for the school in sport or representing it in any other way should be regarded as a distinction and should be recognised as such by the authorities. Everyone should appear in a school stage show at some time or other. The rising excitement that precedes these performances and the deep simple joy of the theatrical experience should be enjoyed to the full.

Some teachers especially obsessed with the maximum passes in the external exams will frown on these activities because they distract pupils from their studies. There is little substance in such arguments as long as the school preserves a sensible balance between work and play. Teenage children have an almost inexhaustible reserve of energy and have no difficulty in keeping half-a-dozen activities going, provided that they are interested. Adults lack this dynamic gusto and assume that the pupils are as easily exhausted as they themselves.

For new entrants, social occasions should be organised by the houses to encourage the pupils to make as many acquaintances as possible from their own year. These events should take place in the evening and parents should attend. The children may act as hosts.

On great school occasions — like the annual concert or a football final or an excursion or a swimming gala — the build-up should be such that most of the pupils would wish to be present.

As a picture of the school is forming in the minds of the younger pupils, notions of service and of loyalty should take shape. Occasionally their services should be called on to help one or other of the many charities in aid of those suffering from destitution or disease at home or abroad. At other times the appeal will be for some project to benefit their own school community, a drive for funds for their outdoor centre or to purchase a minibus. In such ways the idea of citizenship, of responsibility stretching beyond self-interest, is nurtured:

> *'Heaven doth with us as we with torches do,*
> *Not light them for themselves.'*

Loyalty is a conception not favoured much nowadays. To many it smacks of the abhorred 'old school tie'. But it has a long, luminous history in life and literature. It is one of Shakespeare's virtues:

> *'He that can endure*
> *To follow with allegiance a fall'n lord*
> *Does conquer him that did his master conquer*
> *And earns a place i' the story.'*

Loyalty implies constancy, reliability, the satisfaction of sharing labour and hardship with good comrades. Its opposites are fickleness and treachery. School loyalty means supporting the team, participating in school efforts or projects, putting school occasions, engagements and commitments high on the list of one's priorities. It also means, if the school is a real family, that pupils will not denigrate their school to strangers, or take stories of internal happenings to press reporters or of trivial injustices to parents. Good families do not 'wash their dirty linen in public'. The corollary to this principle is, of course, that the school will be so governed that such occasions for complaint are rare.

Self-criticism is all important for the health of the school, or any institution, and there should be no lack of occasions for staff and pupils to ventilate grievances internally. But all must beware of the guileful reporter who inveigles children into making statements which may be used to discredit the school. On such occasions the pupils should know that the investigator should be referred to the headmaster who, if he is wise, will shun the conventional 'no comment' response and make frank, balanced, well-considered statements to press and parents when the situation calls for such.

The outward symbol of school loyalty is the wearing of the school uniform. Modern educationists are mainly against it. Abolition is one of the planks in the political policy of 'pupil-power'. The arguments of the abolitionists seem to be, first, that the wearing of uniform is an authoritarian means of emphasising the master/slave relationship of staff and pupils; second, that it limits the field of personal preference, of expressing individuality, of the right to choose; third, that it emphasises social or economic or class distinctions (since, they argue, the poorer child cannot afford a uniform), and this, in turn, widens the gap between the two nations in the school and helps to create rebels.

The last of these arguments is certainly not valid. In most secondary schools practically all the first year intake are dressed in school uniform; it is about the end of second year that many pupils abandon it. (Incidentally, the clothes chosen to replace the uniform are usually every bit as expensive.) The change in dress betokens a change of attitude to the school. The desire to change over to something 'trendy', or to garments typifying adherence to some teenage pop cult, has become stronger than loyalty to the school. Or to put it another way — the school has not proved itself good enough to deserve the pupil's loyalty. The change represents a challenge to the school. If the school can present itself to the pupils as an honourable commonwealth, where all are of equal status and the needs of all are cared for, if it is happy, vigorous and prolific of opportunities for rich, full living at a multitude of levels, academic, recreational, aesthetic and social, then the pupils will not discard the uniform which they wore proudly on the day of enrolment as citizens of 'no mean city'.

The argument that pupils wish to express their individuality by choosing their own school dress is unconvincing. If they must so express themselves, they have every evening and weekend to do so. To change dress at such times may heighten the pleasure by contrast. This so-called urge to express their individuality in dress is not at all apparent when hundreds of them adopt the colours of the local team on Saturday afternoons, or when they willingly accept the uniform of Boys' Brigade or Scouts or Guides or Army Cadets or the local brass band or the dress of the pop group in which they play or indeed when they change en masse into jeans, the uniform of dissident youth. So far from expressing their personalities by dress they mostly seem ready to accept all sorts of uniforms or badges to identify themselves with clubs, societies, cults, etc. The question is not whether self-expression should be encouraged, it is rather whether their school is important to them.

The economic argument need not detain us. Many schools have a system by which blazers, in good condition, are handed in, cleaned and sold to pupils as a normal happening with no social stigma involved.

The argument that school uniform is a means of maintaining slavish obedience to the staff has no basis in reality. Thousands of sports organisations in the land have their own individual blazers and ties, social clubs have their badges, our international teams, for any kind of contest, sally forth immaculately uniformed and one could extend the list of examples indefinitely. In no one of these cases could it be argued that the object was authoritarian. One wears a uniform to express not subservience but pride in being a member of an honourable institution. So it is with school uniform, or should be. But perhaps pride is one of the emotions that the sociologists wish to outlaw from schools. It is suspect; it is the language of the heart, not the clinic.

There are many advantages in the wearing of school uniform. As the pupils move from school into the shopping centre of the town, their presence is recognised by members of the public, and the school becomes a visible component of the larger community, a positive element not to be ignored. The pupils know that the tone of their school is in high repute; there may be an element of pride in being identified with it.

Within the school the wearing of uniforms nullifies any inclination a pupil might have had to 'show off' by wearing expensive clothing or by sporting the bizarre outfits of the pop cult currently in vogue.

Those who support the right of pupils to come to school in casual dress are really arguing for casualness in work and in behaviour. Appropriately dressed people, neat and trim, look as if they mean business and suggest efficiency and professionalism. Is there anything wrong with school pupils looking (and, one hopes, feeling) the same? Our society can hardly be thought to have benefited from twenty years of casualness.

A good school punctuates the session by a number of traditional occasions, some of which involve an element of ceremony, some internal, others public. There may be religious services, inauguration of office-bearers, closing ceremonies. The impact of these memorable occasions may be aesthetically enhanced by the colour of a thousand uniforms. That same beauty transforms the drabbest school corridor as the columns move from room to room. Thus will the school be remembered far in the future.

The main argument in favour of uniform is that its use confirms the feeling of school fellowship, the occupancy of common ground, the sense of the warmth of friendship, company on the journey. Many of our fellow human beings would give a lot for that.

The overriding problem in the comprehensive school is the fusion of the two worlds of the academic élite and the unintellectual mass. Until such time as the curriculum is reformed the main hope lies in the extra-curricular activities. These should be developed to the full, the emphasis being put on such clubs and societies as would be likely to appeal to the average and sub-average pupil. The policy should be that every pupil should join at least one activity and that every effort should be made to keep him involved in it throughout his school career. The benefits that accrue from the various activities will be dealt with later. What is worth emphasising at the moment is that the pupils should be making the main contribution to the operation of these activities, instead of being 'spoon-fed' by the staff organiser. Pupil committees should be the normal way of managing clubs and societies, selecting teams, etc. Obligations should be laid on members — to make decisions, to fulfil duties, to create, to serve. These functions should be part of the school lifestyle, the school experience. And pupils should be encouraged if they propose to found new activities on their own, provided these are practicable propositions.

An ultra-conservative attitude to innovations initiated by pupils often provokes a cynical us-and-them attitude. If new ideas proliferate and new customs take root, the first reaction of the staff should be one of interest rather than of automatic condemnation. The deadness and the artificiality of many schools arise from the vain assumption that established routine is enough. The essence of life is change and this must be accepted as the truth about the school community. School is not just a patterned preparation for life — it is life itself. What is more, it ought to be a life worth living, full of vitality, excitement, novelty, experiment, imagination, emotion, surprise, humour. It should be a fascinating world, a splendid spectacle, a colourful pageant, a rich story unfolding day by day. No two days will be alike. There will be the stable elements, the timetable, the routines, the exams, the traditional events, which the rolling year brings round. Over against these will be the new happenings which, at the least, might provide talking points in the playground conversations for a day or two, before passing into oblivion. Other initiatives might carry the seed of greater permanence. A group of seniors might found a weekly news sheet; a troupe of pupil buskers, armed with guitars, might mount open-air displays at intervals in some sheltered nook in the playground; some Sixth Year eccentrics might form themselves into a Victorian Club and apply for permission to play croquet on the lawn of one of the quadrangles; some second year girls might open a swap shop in aid of War on Want. A chess or table-tennis league, involving both staff and senior pupils, might come into existence. An application might come from a group of pupils for the use of the school hall every Friday evening for disco or bingo. An intellectual coterie might initiate poetry reading sessions in the library at lunchtime. Where you have originality, audacity and a surplus of energy, there is little limit to what you might devise.

It is a pity if members of the staff habitually frown on all such innovations as unnecessary disturbances of routine. Each new vogue is an attempt to satisfy the need of the inherently discontented human spirit. The proper enlightened attitude would be to ask if there were any real harm in the proposed innovation. Otherwise let it go on; wish it luck; offer help if one can. It will then become another school tradition surviving until it is replaced by another innovation answering to changed times and circumstances or it might just die an early death.

In either case the innovation will have added another thread to the multicoloured skein which is the school experience.

As with every aspect of school government, the crux is the point of balance between discipline and freedom. The responsibility accepted by head and staff to ensure good order and safety for all the pupils does not mean that education is a matter of conditioning pupils to certain modes of behaviour. Pupils of unusual interests, those who have a flair for floating original ideas, those who have distinct and unusual qualities of personality, those with the gift of leading and persuading others, must be encouraged to play their part in the community, developing their own talents and contributing something of value to school life. Generally what such pupils need is not restraint but guidance. If they can come to think of themselves as having a part to play in the shaping of the lifestyle of the school, of enriching it with their own gifts, then we shall be a few steps nearer to the creation of the good commonwealth.

A quite different problem is that of the pupil with the gift of leadership and the strong personality but corrupt in morals, perverse in will. Such a one can set himself up as a centre of opposition to the policies of the authorities. He finds satisfaction in winning over to his own behavioural patterns pupils who would, normally, be co-operative and reliable. He may attract to himself a coterie of his fellows, similarly antisocial. The group may select some youth of transparent innocence and entice him into their circle, quite deliberately. It is a sad business to see the coarsening of the characters and personalities of children who, when they enrolled, were conspicuous for the refinement of their manners. When such groups of unscrupulous activists are organised they become centres of delinquency and insubordination. Mischief is their norm and those who will not join them are subject to derision and even physical bullying. The solution is not easy. Quick recognition of the malaise is essential for the innocent must be insulated in some way from the temptations of the persuaders. But this is a negative approach. The persuaders themselves must be put under the microscope to see whether their personal dynamism might not be sublimated in the interests of the whole society.

If we are to model the school on the conception of a family, the building must be looked on as a home. In most schools there are house recreation rooms. The supervision of these and the prevention of needless damage should be the responsibility of pupils, with house staff never far away just as, in a good home, the mother is generally on hand to be appealed to in case of accident or disagreement. Efforts should be made to have these recreational rooms available for use for an hour after school closes. Any arrangements that induce children to remain in their school after the official working hours should be welcomed. The more frequently the pupils are present in games room or corridor, the more quickly will sheer familiarity and habit give birth to the affection which can make one's schooling a profound experience. Later, in memory, the sensuous aspect of the school interior will acquire a visionary quality: the murals, the rolls of honour on the walls, the network of corridors, young voices in friendly altercation, the laughter of girls.

The experience that can hardly fail to arouse a pupil's feeling for his school and the fellowship it offers is that of finding himself in the school building for some function, on a cold winter evening. The corridors look mysterious in the unaccustomed artificial light. The place suddenly suggests hidden meanings. Unfamiliar shadows, eerie silence where normally there is clamour, echoes of footsteps accentuated by the silence, all this is food for the imagination. The familiar has grown slightly unreal, perhaps romantic. An aura has descended. The disagreeable noises of daytime, the hostile authoritative voices have vanished. These have been replaced by an alluring mellowness, welcoming, satisfying, the climate of affection. Usually nocturnal visits to the school are occasioned by an enjoyable function, a school party, a film, the annual concert, opera or play, an exhibition of art or craft, a parent-pupil meeting. It may dawn on a pupil suddenly that this is not the forbidding habitat of discipline and drudgery: this is home.

Kipling has described the experience in his poem on Sussex:

'So to the land our heart we give
Till the sure magic strike,
And memory, use and love make live
Us and our fields alike.'

Certain rooms and areas have their own special significance.

Noticeboards are important. These are focal points of communication, the starting place for animated conversations, the beginning of adventures on the sportsfield, the realisation of dreams.

One can tell a lot about a school from a perusal of the notices. Apart from the information they give about the amount and nature of the extra-curricular activities (bingo in the school hall at four o'clock) they let the reader know whether the school is seriously in business. Are notices signed? Dated? Removed when out of date? Spelt correctly? Free from facetiousness? Fully informative? Neatly spaced out? Free from addenda contributed quite unofficially by the notorious clown of class three? Some senior pupil should look after that noticeboard. It is a kind of information mart, fraught with tidings of serious import, of joy and despair, of tears and quickened pulse, the birthplace of fabulous achievements. Membership of the school community suddenly becomes real.

Another centre of communal activity should be the school library. Pupils, whether engaged in projects or in research for Sixth Year Studies dissertations, may very properly frequent the library making it an academic cloister:

> *'Let my due feet* [says Milton] *never fail*
> *To walk the studious cloister's pale.'*

For those with intellectual or cultural inclinations this should be a joyful retreat. Scholars love the feel of a new book and the librarian should be glad to display her latest acquisitions to those not averse to enlightenment. One can imagine the library being the venue for discussion groups, literary societies, poetry readings and play readings at lunchtime or after four. It should be a brightly lit and comfortably furnished room, colourfully postered with notices about cultural activities in the school and in the town. The dominance of radio and TV, as vehicles for mental enrichment and the acquisition of ideas and knowledge, places the reading habit in jeopardy. Children nowadays read badly and read slowly. The library should be the base for a crusade for literacy, for the appreciation of books, for the spread of the habit. Near or within the library there should be a school bookshop, new and secondhand. To the modern child a shop is an irresistible magnet, a factor in his social life. Open a bookshop in a school and you will have no lack of customers. It will be the focal point for those who love books and a forum for civilised dialogue.

A civilised and civilising centre, in another way, should be the dining hall. If consideration of the rights of others is part of the school code of conduct, the dining room is the place where one should see the precept in action. A brief, meaningful and intelligible grace should remind the thoughtful of the sacramental aspect of sharing one's bread with brothers and sisters. The departure of ceremony from the modern school shows the extent to which the cheapness, shallowness and meaninglessness of modern life now pervade our school societies.

In some schools the population are obliged, or at least expected, to vacate the buildings at morning and afternoon intervals and at lunchtime and go into extensive areas, traditionally called playgrounds. Valuable for providing opportunities for breathing fresh air and getting exercise, they can be dangerous places. It is in these wide campuses, usually too extensive for supervision, that the depraved and the malevolent find scope for their designs. In such areas tendencies to violence or vandalism may be exercised with impunity, not to speak of vices of greater turpitude. The trend now is to provide leisure areas, roofed enclosures, cloisters and common rooms which provide comfort, protection against bad weather and encouragement to behave to acceptable standards. If the corporate life of the school is vigorous and multiplex, part of the lunchtime interval will be fully used in conducting clubs and other activities.

To some minds, school playgrounds will suggest pupil politics and the agitations that may accompany this phenomenon. One hears, from time to time, of playground meetings, pupil walk-outs, protest rallies and strikes over issues which may be real or simulated. The current strike mania has hit even the most decorous of professions, medical, legal, civil service, higher education and, of course, teaching. This is the world we live in. Should pupils be allowed to protest in this open way? Has striking come to be the universal and completely acceptable machinery for dialogue about differences between contracting parties?

Presumably many teachers, if they were honest, would have to answer in the affirmative. Teachers who have themselves taken part in walk-outs, work-to-rule and strikes, cannot justifiably complain if their pupils use the same tactics in dealing with the school authorities. Shakespeare, as usual, summed it up:

> 'We do but teach
> Bloody instructions which being taught return
> To plague the inventor.'

All sorts of issues are raised by the question. Those who manage schools must maintain good order on the school premises because the physical safety of the pupils is involved and head and teachers cannot avoid responsibility for that. On the other hand, uncompromising suppression of actions aimed at the expression of legitimate grievances may seem unfair and oppressive; it will probably diminish the morale of the school as a whole. But what about the school's public image? The spectacle of a hundred vociferous pupils chanting contumacious slogans in the playground, when they should be filing meekly into classrooms, will bring local reporters scurrying to the scene, a development which may be precisely what the organisers of the demonstration desired.

It is in the handling of such situations that the head's powers of judgement and resourcefulness will be put to the test.

First of all, he should be well aware of grievances long before these occasion public revolt. He should be conversant with pupil opinion on topical issues, as for example, changes in the school rules or other unpopular actions by teachers or by himself. His attitude to the new situation should not be invariably inflexible. Any man who imagines himself to be infallible is unfit to govern. It may be that the action or the decision that sparked off the demonstration was the product of impulse, possibly of ill temper. As I have already argued, new proposals affecting pupils should have been ventilated, argued over and canvassed, long before they were validated. If this had been done and the pupils know that their point of view has been fairly considered, there will be small likelihood of precipitate action. And obstinacy in a headmaster is not necessarily a virtue. If, on examination of the pupils' arguments, he sees sense in them, he may well reverse a decision. This need not be interpreted as weakness; it may well enhance the respect in which he is held.

Yet occasionally, even in the best managed school, misunderstandings may produce a confrontation. In dealing with such a demonstration or revolt one must consider the numbers taking part and the type of pupils they are.

Some playground demonstrations are lighthearted replicas of those currently taking place in other schools and reported in the media. A trivial grievance is spotlighted by some spirited youth disposed to enjoy a bit of excitement and, with a few like-minded associates, he passes the word round for a staged protest assembly. Such an uprising presents little danger if the authorities do not over-react. A lighthearted response to a lighthearted ploy will restore normality — a sense of humour and a turn of wit are not least of the assets of an ideal headmaster. The squib will be defused with little risk to the image of the school and the humour engendered by the diversion will brighten the mood of the school for the remainder of the afternoon. It would be made clear to the participants that a repeat performance would come into the category of indiscipline.

Very different in nature would be a playground revolt deliberately initiated and masterminded by habitual militants with political aspirations, the apostles of 'pupil power'. Such episodes adhere to the model of student revolts at universities. The sequence of the stages in such an operation reveals its real purpose, which is not to have a grievance redressed but simply to promote disorder. The decision to organise the protest comes first. After you have settled the details of the operation, you search for a grievance about which to protest. Any grievance will do. This is the format for student militancy and pupil power apes its sponsors, the university dissidents. The complaints, the grievances, the objections put into the mouths of the pupils are not authentic. They savour of left-wing doctrinaire theorising and, like most products of that source, are absurdly unrealistic. The grievances are of the kind a theorist, ignorant of school realities, might imagine to be issues in the school, religious assemblies, uniform, corporal punishment, whereas if you asked typical pupils to think of grievances they would be more likely to complain about school meals, the lack of school buses in a housing scheme, the preponderance of homework given by a certain department. The grievances are used merely as pretexts for creating disorder and advancing the political careers of the school dissidents serving an apprenticeship in militancy.

Pupils' unions do not seem to have made much headway in Scotland and one doubts if they have a future. With the rapid turnover in personnel, leadership is discontinuous so that there is no accumulation of political expertise. The strike weapon, the work to rule and other forms of action are inappropriate as bargaining weapons, for the only people hurt by such action would be the pupils themselves, missing lessons and examinations. Nor can there be any real danger in a school movement that finds its strength not in the grass roots but in adult political agencies. Pupil power is normally no more than a nuisance but if there are activists, capable of prolonged campaigning, rigorous suppression might be necessary, particularly when the militants are being openly encouraged by outside agencies. Those who would set the idea of the class war against the school's philosophy of concord and fellowship would have to be neutralised. The head must denounce their whole wretched philosophy unequivocally, at the risk, inevitably, of being stigmatised as reactionary or fascist.

Our distrust of extremist pupil politicians should not, however, blind us to the wider question of how far pupils might be involved in decision-making. This is a democratic era when workers' representatives take a crucial part in industrial decisions and many educationists believe that pupils should have a similar part to play in the management of schools if for no other purpose than to educate them for the part they will have to take in industrial relations later on in their adult life. Many schools have established school councils, with pupil representatives from every school year sitting beside members of staff with the headmaster as chairman or, in schools recklessly progressive, a pupil in that position.

There is much to be said in favour of such school councils. Their existence allows pupils with ideas to contribute these to the development of school policies and institutions and provides a forum where pupils have the chance to explain to the adults how things look from their angle. It is an answer to the pupils' oft-repeated bitter complaint, 'They never listen to you'.

I have already suggested that if staff and pupils are in continuous dialogue in playground, classroom, corridor and dining hall, there will be a great growth of mutual understanding and many decisions will be based on a consensus of opinion representing the views of the whole community. But there will be many who will not accept this informal type of consultation as truly democratic and would prefer the more formal, legalistic machinery of a council.

However, there are serious difficulties in the operation of this system. For one thing it cannot be truly democratic for, at the end of the day, the head is legally responsible for everything that happens in the school. But staff-pupil relations will certainly not benefit if the head steps in to veto a decision of the council and the various delegates have the task of explaining this outcome to the pupils whom they represent.

This, of course, raises another problem. Have the members to be delegates speaking for the year they represent, or are they to vote on an issue according to their individual judgements?

The head will probably start off by defining the functions of the council as being purely advisory and this will be a difficult notion for the pupil members to accept, particularly the serious-minded ones who are genuinely interested in having a personal share in school government.

To give the council some standing, the head will permit it to settle certain questions which he, privately, does not think of much importance. Even here, where there is real decision-making, the senior members of the council will not be happy about the first and second year representatives having the same voting powers as themselves. There is certainly something absurd in immature, inexperienced twelve-year-olds having the same voting powers as eighteen-year-old seniors or as teacher members of the council, some of them perhaps in their sixties.

Nevertheless the school council is a useful forum for sounding school opinion but there is some danger in having the council meeting regularly at specific statutory times. Sometimes the meeting is convened when there is nothing of importance on the agenda. To justify the meeting an item of a trivial nature is given much more attention than it deserves. The result is that much talking about it causes it to escalate until it attains the importance of a major issue, distracting attention from more important things and generating some bad temper as well. If there are to be school councils, let them be summoned only when there is a question of some importance to be discussed; and let the head make it plain, at the outset, whether he is asking merely for advice or whether the decision of the council, no matter what it is, will be binding. But often all his diplomacy will be needed to retain the support of the more independently minded members. There is always a faint suggestion of deceit about school councils, a reluctance to proclaim the indubitable fact that no decision of theirs will be implemented if the headmaster is opposed to it.

The most serious weakness of school councils is just that some of the members have not attended the school long enough to be attuned to its traditions and the subtle refinements of its lifestyle. They are not yet on the wavelength. That is why pupil participation in decision-making should involve senior pupils only. They have experienced whatever is unique and characteristic in the school climate and will have acquired the instinct for assessing which new developments or innovations will harmonise with the features they know so well.

Chapter 11

The Sixth Year

The Sixth Year, in many schools, is an academic élite group, entry to which is conditional upon having previously attained a reasonable academic standard. This is shortsighted policy. In order that the Sixth may be able to play the part in the life of the school for which their experience of the school has equipped them, they should have the strength of a closely knit squad, composed of friends of long standing and bound together by chains of shared experience. Nothing whatever is to be gained by selection on pedantic, academic grounds and a great deal is lost, notably loyalty and good will.

The term 'The Sixth' as used here refers to the group of pupils who are in the last year of a full academic course and are, by reason of length of service, recognised as in a special category.

The most important offices in the school should, in the main, be held by Sixth Year pupils. It is absurd to have prefects appointed from Fifth and Fourth years. How can they be expected to wield any sort of authority over pupils two years their senior?

Similarly, if there are elections for appointment to such offices, the franchise should be limited to senior years, Fifth and Sixth, possibly Fourth for some offices, but never any lower. Seldom do pupils have any close knowledge of those in other years and an election in which one's knowledge of the candidates is nil or, at most, based on hearsay or on a reputation in sport, is little better than drawing the names out of a hat.

I am assuming that the Sixth are the group in the school most to be trusted by reason of their background. They have been there for a very long time. If these boys and girls by the time they reach that final year have not formed a deep respect for the school, have not become completely familiar with its habitual processes and its traditions, have not come to accept the ethos of the school, have not learned to serve it faithfully and to safeguard its honour, if they cannot be trusted to maintain its accepted standards of behaviour, to contribute by speech and action to the improvement of its moral climate — if the Sixth have not learned all these things, then the head and his staff have failed to fulfil their supreme duty — to transmit to their charges a vision of good citizenship.

But if the Sixth have acquired such concepts and are actuated by them in their own school lives, then they will be fit to play a significant part in the consultative processes and in the decision-making concerned with the day-to-day life of the community.

It should not be forgotten that since fourth year leavers are, in the main, only moderately endowed intellectually, the average intelligence of the Sixth will be higher than that of other years. A school would be all the poorer intellectually, socially and morally, if there were no Sixth and perhaps even more so if there were no Fifth.

The Sixth, for those who are prepared to take it, is the most important year in the school. To the members of the year, all that has gone before in their secondary school lives will have been a preparation for it. Its success is apparent when one hears (as one often does) the Sixth Year pupil say, 'This year has been quite unlike any other year that has gone before it. I can't explain it, but it has definitely been the best.'

And just as pupils will benefit in a score of ways from having taken the sixth year, the school will likewise benefit from their leadership and the example they set. They will have a significant contribution to make to the moral climate of the school. If a school can do anything to develop character, then that intangible but real attribute will be discernible in these boys and girls, now possessed of all their school has to offer and ready to transmit it to others.

These finished products of the school should be an élite group. From the ranks should emerge the professional men and women who will eventually take key positions in commerce, industry, medicine and law. They will find careers in the media, in the theatre, music and literature and other arts, in social service, public administration, in commissioned rank in the services, in the church and philanthropic service abroad. They will provide society with its teachers, lecturers and professors, people who stand for elected positions in public life, who will be well known, who will be watched closely and listened to. What they say and how they say it will be norms on which people will model their own attitudes and conduct. If our society is to recover its health and its spirit, the quality of the Sixth Year pupils of the schools will be a crucial factor. The essence of professional eminence should be there and if we ignore their potential we are neglecting their own rights and the future needs of our society.

Schools would be well advised to pay more attention to the question of having a viable Sixth Year, for at the moment, the number of pupils staying for that final year is in decline. The establishment of the teachers' contract, by which the upper limit of pupils in a class was arbitrarily fixed, was educationally counterproductive. The contract in many cases posed, for the headmasters, problems of deployment of staff and these problems were frequently solved by simply abolishing the Sixth Year sections. Sixth Year pupils came to be neglected, often sitting at the back of junior classes or idling in common room or library. It was understandable that they should consider this a waste of time.

As for faith, the schools will have to define, emphatically, the social and moral ends that the Sixth Year would achieve. They will have to believe that the final year has something special, even unique, to offer, an aim that will embrace academic, social and moral aspects of education. They will have to emphasise that the Sixth is a time to mature socially in the company of one's school year; to learn to accept and to carry out responsible roles; to exercise leadership of the younger pupils; to exemplify standards of loyalty and service; to grow up into the kind of people who will not only know how to live fully and richly but will be assets to the adult community which they are about to enter.

What has got to be removed is the picture of the Sixth Year as a life of privilege and ease. To be offered, instead, will be study in depth of specialist subjects, 'taster courses' of new subjects and a field of rewarding service to the school in the company of companions of five years' standing.

The courses offered in Sixth Year will be varied and complex. Top-class scholars will concentrate on reaching advanced levels in their main subjects; others will still be seeking certificate passes for entrance to tertiary education; some may be attracted to new subjects out of interest, to broaden their intellectual horizons or to add a complementary element to specialist subjects already followed. In other cases a cognate subject may be added, an extra language to the linguist, an extra science to the scientist, economics and accounting to the intending lawyer, statistics to those seeking careers in public administration, shorthand to the budding reporter. In the number of subjects carried, the Sixth Year course would be less exacting than the Fifth but the chosen subjects would be studied in depth. The master or mistress in charge would be one well fitted to guide these studies with a view to long-term objectives, a teacher of engaging personality but not devoid of drive. Purposeful private study in a reading room or library, as a preparation for university modes, would be a feature of the course

and most of the subjects studied should have examination objectives —
Certificate of Sixth Year Studies, GCE A-level, Bursary or
Scholarship competitions. The criticism that Sixth Year is
academically a waste of time must be answered.

Curricular policies do not, however, constitute the matter of this
book. What contribution should Sixth Year make to the social and
moral health of the body politic?

The question of privilege and of liberation from the disciplinary
restrictions of school life will be a prior consideration, as it is with the
advocates of the Sixth Year College. But this aspect cannot be
divorced from a group of kindred conceptions: service, duty and
responsibility. If the Sixth are to be allowed the privilege of free,
unsupervised time in the course of the day, this would largely be to give
them the opportunity to carry out the various duties assigned to them
for service to the school.

Plans, in operation in some quarters, to modify normal school
discipline in the case of the Sixth seem largely to ignore the duties that
should be the corollary of privilege. Under the system I refer to, Sixth
Year students may leave school, when they have no classes, and go
'down town' for coffee or snooker if they so desire. This practice
would seem to operate unfairly and be open to abuse. The number of
free periods available for this kind of privileged relaxation would vary
enormously among individuals, according to the courses they were
following. Pupils not legitimately free would be tempted to join
friends indulging in their legitimate privilege. Over-use of the
concession might cause administrative inconvenience as most of the
Sixth would have key roles in the organisation of corporate activities
and ought, really, to be available for business arising therefrom. The
privilege I have been discussing, if granted, should be specifically
limited so that all should have the same amount of this freedom. And
one wonders whether, in the present state of industry and commerce,
we are really conferring a benefit on our country by accustoming
young men and women to walk out for recreational satisfaction in the
middle of the working day. A visit, between ten and twelve a.m., to
city coffee houses, resorts frequented by slick businessmen 'fleeting the
time carelessly as they did in the golden world', will confirm my
reservations about the custom.

It is more useful to think of the Sixth as a special group rather than a
privileged one. To mark this separateness they should have a comfortable, well-appointed room of their own, which they would use more,
perhaps, as a base from which to conduct the management of their

various activities than as a retreat for indolent ease. The separateness of this room is crucial. No pupil below the Sixth, no teacher and no headmaster should enter it unless by invitation. There is nothing revolutionary about such a restriction. In the Army, the Sergeants' Mess is similarly sacrosanct; officers do not enter unless invited. The effect on morale of this authorised privacy for the Sixth is tremendous. They feel that they are being treated with respect, something about which young people of their age are very sensitive. They have received the confidence of headmaster and teachers. They have a retreat where, in reasonable comfort, they can enjoy one another's company and talk freely, without the inhibitions that accompany dialogue with authority. The crux of the situation is that the management of the room and the kind of conduct permitted there are at their own discretion. They are confronted, fairly and squarely, with the obligation to evaluate different modes of behaviour, to control the wilder, anti-social impulses, to which all adolescents are occasionally subject, and to conduct themselves with due regard to their status in the school.

Anyone who has had experience of the behaviour patterns of adolescents will know that occasionally there will be instances of horseplay (the word beloved by acidic headmasters), and damage to furniture and rumours of smoking and gambling, and worse, in the Sixth Year common room. This is a situation that has occurred in every school that possesses such a common room and, I am afraid, the method of dealing with the misdemeanour is a stock reaction, a drama featuring a bustling red-faced headmaster in the key role. He bursts into the room at an interval, breathing fire and slaughter. He calls his Sixth Year pupils hooligans, irresponsible vandals, guttersnipes, accuses them of behaving like first year pupils, raising his voice pro-gressively to an apex of stridency that makes every pupil within earshot shudder, and finally orders the whole group out of the room (often in the hearing of juniors who, up to that point, had held the Sixth in veneration), declaring that it will be closed until the end of the session. What this irascible man has gained by his outburst and his melo-dramatic expulsion performance, apart from the preservation of a few articles of furniture, it would not be easy to conjecture. What he has lost is more obvious — the loyalty, co-operation and the service of those who should have been his best friends.

Such episodes (and they are not uncommon) only serve to show that some heads do not understand senior pupils and do not have the remotest idea of how to handle them. The axiom that the head has forgotten, if indeed he ever knew it, is that one does not humiliate

Sixth Year pupils. Presumably there will be a head boy and a head girl, or a school captain or a head monitor, who should have been elected by his contemporaries. It should be sufficient, in the case I have described, for the head to call that elected leader to his room, inform him that he has heard rumours of unacceptable conduct in the common room and tell the pupil that he had better do something about it. The latter will act because he knows it is his duty. He will call a meeting and describe the situation. Those concerned will apologise if that is necessary and make amends in other ways. You may say that there is no certainty that the pupils concerned will behave in that satisfactory way. The answer is that it is nearly certain, for the head pupil, presumably, will be one who does not shirk unpleasant duties and the pupils, presumably, will value the friendship of the headmaster and the reputation of the Sixth Year group. For this is the kind of pupils the headmaster will have if he has taken care of their moral education up through the school; if he has conveyed to them the importance of honesty and responsibility and courage; if he has nurtured feelings of respect for the school and the duty to preserve its good name. But the headmaster will not have pupils of this quality if he thinks that a school can be managed by remote control from an isolated cell and by ignoring the thoughts and feelings of the thousand pupils supposedly in his care.

But such situations are delicately poised on a certain contingency — that the head has had the courage to grant to his Sixth Year pupils the privilege of privacy in their common room. Their appreciation of this gesture and their awareness of being trusted will be a guarantee of an honourable response to a complaint about their conduct.

Trustfulness, not discipline, should be the key to the relationship between headmaster and staff on the one hand and the Sixth Year on the other. The latter should be regarded not as pupils but as junior partners with the staff in the handling of problems and activities in the school. For this is the time for action — the moment in their school career when all notions they have acquired about service and reliability and duty and civilised behaviour will become reality, not talk, not open-ended discussion groups in classrooms, but action based on the values they have acquired during five years in a spiritually healthy community.

The kind of service which the Sixth Year might give would vary according to the needs of the school and the talents of individual pupils. The gifted scholars, working hard at academic objectives, would not be expected to perform the same kind of service as those whose scholarship aims were more modest. Their contribution would be more tenuous, more refined. It would be, in short, keeping the flame of learning alive in the school, learning not as a means to an end, as it is with most pupils, but learning simply for its own sake, the study of subjects for no other reason than, like Mount Everest, because they are there. Scholarship is at a low ebb in our schools because we have become so mercenary minded. Even our most able pupils think of their subjects as nothing more than doors opening on lucrative careers and the minds of the students are occupied not so much by a divine curiosity to learn more and more, as by cynical calculation of how much work to do to attain a certain grade of pass in the exams. What, sadly, is not realised is that the search for knowledge is a glorious end in itself. To be lost in the profundities of a subject is a kind of timeless experience, one of the deepest sources of bliss ever discovered by man. 'Studies serve for delight' is the opening statement of Bacon's most famous essay on the subject and there is no more to be said. Now if there are scholars of that old-fashioned kind in our Sixth Year, then they are serving the school splendidly by their mere presence. I do not speak of the honour such students might bring to the school by winning scholarships and high places in bursaries competitions, though a school would, rightly, take pride in such distinctions. The importance of their presence is just that they attract into their company other pupils of similar inclinations; they strengthen one another; they exchange ideas; they communicate an aura of culture that will perhaps evoke wonder and interest in their fellow-pupils. The school library will be their haunt; their mentors the most accomplished scholars on the staff — minds subtle and refined. 'The light shines in the darkness and the darkness does not extinguish it.'

There are, however, a host of more commonplace services that the Sixth Year will perform for their school.

In dress and bearing they will show an example to all others. They will be regular and punctual in attendance. If they smoke or drink it will not be in public. Whatever their habits are in respect of these weaknesses, they should co-operate with staff in outlawing them on the school premises. They should accept duties of surveillance in the playground. To carry these out they may have to show courage.

If they have ability in any school sport, they should place it at the service of the school. In sport they should set an example in obedience to the rules, self-control and the magnanimous gesture to the opposing sides. They should be involved in the school show, on stage, or backstage or front of the house.

In character-building courses, they should assist younger pupils by advice and encouragement. They should be leaders in adventurous projects.

They should be first to volunteer for disagreeable jobs like shifting furniture, the erection of tents, the washing of dishes on special school occasions like parents' social evenings or garden fêtes. Leadership and lowly service co-exist in the lives of the best people. This is a Christian conception.

They should co-operate with the guidance staff in trying to solve the problems of young unstable pupils, habitual truants, the shy, the frightened, the wayward. A useful service is to call at the home of such a one and accompany him to school.

They should preside at meetings of pupils' debating societies or school councils. They should act as secretaries of clubs and societies. They should take it in turn to do reception duties at the school entrance, welcoming strangers with appropriate courtesy and guiding them to their destination.

One of the Sixth should be on duty in the anteroom to the head's office, to perform tasks that might involve visits to remote areas of the school. On occasions they might work with the head on some special task. Each pupil would take his turn on a rota system and the head would have an ideal opportunity to get to know these pupils as individuals. A routine part of the head's day would be a five minutes' conversation with the pupil on duty.

Any member of staff who was involved in time-consuming extra-curricular work should be able to enlist the help of a Sixth Year pupil as his special assistant, as for example, preparing programmes for a school show or secretarial work with respect to a school journey or holiday.

Other duties for the Sixth might include the preparation of the magazine and the canvassing for advertisements. They might run school bookshops or tuckshops. Some of them should be in charge of the school noticeboards.

These are but a few examples of the service they might give. Many would argue that the high standards of behaviour expected of them are unrealistic. There certainly will be times when they will grow weary in well-doing and there will also be occasions when some will be guilty of offences against the rules of the school. The head should personally deal with such cases, but not publicly. A heart-to-heart talk in the head's office would be sufficient in less serious cases; for the graver delinquencies a reprimand in the presence of the rest of the Sixth (and of no one else) would be the normal procedure. This is not really a mild sanction. To stand before the headmaster with your friends standing round, silently, in a circle, and to hear your offence objectively described as an infringement of the school's ethical code is an experience not likely to be forgotten. When it is over, the head will instruct all those present to make no further reference to the matter in conversation out in the school. This consideration for the feelings of the delinquent will add to the effectiveness of the reprimand.

Members of the Sixth should be in frequent dialogue with head-master, house master and staff and should be kept informed of matters affecting the school, if these are not of a confidential nature. They should be informed of the identities of visitors to the school; impending changes in the staff; plans for the school's next show; the headmaster's intended absence from duty to attend a conference; the colour scheme decided upon for the repainting of the building. There is no reason in the world why these senior pupils should not be told these things. To be taken into the confidence of the management in this way confirms their status and will strengthen their attachment to the school. It would be a gesture of trust.

Whether or not there is a school council, a wise head will sometimes consult his Sixth, just as he would consult his staff, about school policy and proposed changes in the rules. It is right that the pupils' point of view should be heard, but it is likely to be most useful if it is expressed by the most mature and the most experienced of the pupils. A Sixth Year council seems to me to be a more viable instrument of government than a council which includes representatives from the youngest classes.

One of the most damaging administrative changes in recent years was that which allowed pupils to leave school immediately after the external examinations, i.e. without completing the session. It is now the custom for most of them to slip away unnoticed, ending their school lives 'not with a bang but a whimper'. Sixth Year pupils should be persuaded, if possible, to remain for the final six weeks, giving their school some service in return for what the school has given them and then depart on the last day, ceremoniously, with banners flying.

In a general way it is the presence of the Sixth that is all important. When school events are taking place, a goodly number of the Sixth should always be in the vicinity. They should be there, at hand, to take the initiative if any hitch is likely to occur and, in particular, to play the parts of courteous hosts when parents or the public are present. They will be conspicuous by some special insignia, badge or braid, and the standards of conduct they display will be widely observed. For the younger pupils, observation of how the Sixth conduct themselves will be part of the school experience. In speech and action they will seem to embody the values which are implicit in the school's ethical code.

They should be observed to speak frankly and truthfully; they should be seen to be performing the duties they have contracted to perform; they will not be heard publicly denigrating the school; they should be conspicuous for their good manners; they should be looked up to by the very junior pupils as their helpers and friends; their concern for the reputation of the school, in all fields, should be shown by the quality of their service. Their self-discipline should be rigorous; their devotion to the school unswerving; their probity complete.

All that is ideal. There will be cynics who have found their way into the Sixth. Much of what the pupils read in the syllabus of the English departments is the literature of defeat and surrender, the breeding grounds of cynicism.

The great traditional virtues that used to glorify man's choices and actions, fortitude, loyalty, magnanimity, humility, charity and love are no longer thought of as states to be aspired to, luminous and holy, but rather as illusions, manifestations of a psychological process rather than of a spiritual reality. And the half-baked pupil scientist nurtured on the unbalanced course now, lamentably, almost standard in some schools (Maths, Physics, Chemistry, Biology from third to sixth year) may be disposed to belittle the validity of an ethical code.

Yet the young are not naturally cynical; they will respond with warmth to any appeal to their loyalty, particularly in a school setting for which they have, over the years, developed an ever-growing affection.

Should there be an elaborate hierarchy of office for the seniors — prefects, captains, monitors, etc.? The Sixth certainly should have leaders to keep liaison with the authorities and to take responsibility for maintaining the right relationship between the whole group and the authorities and to take the initiative to amend behavioural short-comings. Let there be boy and girl captains and vice-captains elected by secret ballot and only by their fellows in the year. Younger pupils, in as much as they cannot know the candidates well enough, should never take part in the elections. There are schools where the head or the staff choose such office-bearers. This is the traditional paternalism, the enlightened despotism taking over once more. It is unwise. Neither headmaster nor staff know the pupils as well as they know one another. Sometimes one finds a boy adept at maintaining a pleasing but basically spurious persona for the benefit of the school authorities. But his fellows know the truth about him and their opinion of him is lowered further by their awareness of his calculated acts of deception. It is just possible that the autocratic and ill-informed headmaster might appoint such a one to the captaincy and then wonder at the collapse of morale in the senior school. The head boy or girl must be one who enjoys the respect of his or her fellow-pupils and who can exercise leadership and exert influence. As I have already explained, the obvious method of dealing with unacceptable conduct on the part of the Sixth is to leave the matter in the hands of their leader, who will effect the required solution by a meeting of the group. A teachers' captain or a head-masters' captain would be less able to handle the situation and would fail to achieve an amicable solution.

Should there be a corps of prefects? On the whole, no. With Sixth Year being smaller than in previous years, all members of the Sixth should ipso facto enjoy the status and share the duties that previously belonged to elected prefects. All will appreciate that the whole group are being trusted. In performing their duties considerable freedom of initiative and decision-making will be granted to them. Many of them will unexpectedly mature — grow up with the responsibility. A split Sixth is dangerous — prefects and non-prefects. Some schools have prefects' rooms from which non-prefects are excluded. This is wrong. Entry to the Sixth is a time for unity, not for driving wedges.

Who will be the link between the Sixth and the school authorities? There is a post in many schools: Head of the Upper School. If he is to be guide, philosopher and friend to the Sixth, he has to be good. The egoistic, bullying disciplinarian type will not do. He must be a persuader rather than an autocrat and preferably one who has been on the staff for many years and knows the atmosphere of the place. He must be flexible in his ideas, approachable, a defender of the status and the dignity of the Sixth, an interpreter of the school's ethic to the pupils, a man who has assimilated the atmosphere of the school so completely that he has a sure instinct about how each Sixth Year might contribute to the well-being of the community and enrich its traditions. Ideally the headmaster should be consulted when the head of upper school is appointed. Sometimes the authorities appoint the wrong man, imperfectly understanding the qualities required for the role. There could be no greater calamity than for a complete cynic or a humourless authoritarian to be given charge of the Sixth. If this should happen, it will be the duty of the headmaster to redefine the duties of this promoted post so that the harm of the wrong appointment may be minimised and, in such a case, the head may be obliged to take over many of these duties himself.

Whatever may be arranged for the guidance of the Sixth, the head-master should know each of them by name and should frequently converse with them. They should feel that he is their friend. On school occasions they may very well be treated as if they were teachers, dispensing hospitality, showing visitors around, dignified partners in the establishment. They will not forget the warmth and friendliness with which they were treated in the closing days of their school life. Long afterwards it will be a serene memory.

As to the behavioural standards presented by these senior pupils, one would expect the corps to be an instrument of social education. The word 'tone' is commonly used to describe the communal atmosphere which is apparent to the discerning visitor after only half an hour in the school. The evidence on which conclusions are based are the appearance of the pupils (uniform, tidiness etc.) and their manners. The Sixth will set an example in these respects, help to train younger pupils in the school ethos, showing what individuals will do on specific occasions.

A good Sixth Year pupil will not be in doubt as to the implications of his school's philosophy. It is disturbing to note how, in recent times, the forces working against traditional values have become audacious and positive. We have anti-heroes in plays, 'black' theatre, open admiration in the media for celebrities who are 'brash', 'abrasive', 'sulky', terms which up till recently were derogatory but are not so any more. The fight to preserve standards of civility has now become a very hard battle. But it is worth fighting. 'The gentle mind,' says Spenser, 'by gentle deeds is known,' and the quality of human life can never be enhanced by accepting boorishness, selfishness, insensitivity as norms in our social relations.

It would be profitless to enquire, at this point, whether school environment can create qualities of character. It is enough to believe that, under certain conditions, people can be encouraged and strengthened by their seniors who are close to them. Such closeness is the most obvious feature of a school community. The first stage in the process is for the more mature members of the community, teachers and senior pupils, to realise that they have it within their power to influence others and it may be their duty to do so. And nowhere is this prerequisite inter-relationship more productive than in the field of extra-curricular activities.

Chapter 12

Extra-curricular Activities

Every secondary school offers a range of extra-curricular activities which will vary in number and kind according to the traditions of the school and the availability of teachers to organise them. The timetabled activities presented to the whole school, as part of social education, have already been discussed and we have seen that the success of such schemes is partial because many of the staff are either not inclined to take work outside their own subjects seriously, or their own interests are so limited that they have little to contribute to these hobbies periods.

What we have to look at now are the activities carried on outside school hours (at intervals, in the evenings or on Saturdays) and usually organised by volunteers from the staff who have such enthusiasm for their activity that they are prepared to sacrifice much of their leisure time to promote it in the school. Participation by the pupils is, of course, entirely voluntary and the proportion of the pupils taking part in most schools probably varies between twenty and sixty per cent, seldom more.

For those who do take part, their participation will often provide the most memorable, if not the most productive component of their school experience. Socially this area is a nursery of happiness and friendship; educationally (in the broad sense of preparation, not for careers, but for life), it is a field of infinite potential. To define its educational results (in terms of school activities making people different from what they otherwise would have been) more precisely, would be speculation no more justifiable than forecasting the use that pupils would make, in later life, of the traditional subjects in the curriculum. We shall be on much more secure ground if we examine the corporate life of the school merely as part of the school experience, rather than as an educational experience. The school is not just preparation for life; it is life.

Oddly enough, teachers who organise activities seldom ask themselves why they do it. Probably many of them feel, instinctively, that there are features in most of the activities that bring variety, enrichment and happiness into the lives of pupils who otherwise might be bored or depressed. What are these features?

The variety of clubs, societies and sports, organised in schools, will vary according to the inclinations of staff or pupils at any particular time, but it is usually very great. In short, the athletic range may include football, rugby, hockey, cricket, tennis, table-tennis, basketball, netball, volleyball, golf, shinty, cross-country running, trampolining, judo, boxing, swimming, water-polo, rowing, skiing, canoeing, and many more, each in its own way developing different functions of the human body, each appealing to a particular type of pupil, each demanding its own kind of skill, its appropriate amount of training and coaching, each calling for its own special moral drive from the participants if success is to be achieved.

In another category are the organised hobbies, not demanding physical efforts but a variety of other qualities, skill of hand, mental adroitness, knowledge, experience, patience and enthusiasm. This mixed bag might include aeromodelling, photography, birdwatching, chess, numismatics, philately and angling.

Some activities cater for those who have aesthetic interests or inclinations. We find, nowadays, that many schools have orchestras and silver bands, pipe bands, folksinging and pop groups, dance clubs, choirs, drama clubs, school operatic societies (the last three presenting performances at the end of the session), pottery and painting clubs.

Other societies appeal to the more intellectually inclined: debating societies, school magazines, theatre clubs.

Sometimes there are religious clubs concerned with bible study or discussion of worldwide social and moral issues. Their activities include meetings with speakers from outside the school, films and weekend conferences at religious centres like Iona.

The most academically useful clubs are those related to school subjects. Many schools have French and German clubs where, in the relaxed and comfortable atmosphere of the school on a Friday evening, pupils may assimilate culture and lifestyles of European countries by means of films, records, parties, concerts or talks by the overseas students, all providing an agreeable follow-up to the less colourful material presented to them in the classroom by day. Groups of brilliant senior physics pupils may be at work on a research project, of an original nature, for some national competition. An ardent history teacher may have founded a local history society which will meet in the public library to reconstruct the history of the town from nineteenth-century files. The classics people may form a club to concern itself with antiquities and archaeology. The maths people may do the like with computers. The English Department may sponsor a theatre club and make visits to the theatre, regularly, to keep in touch with modern developments in production and acting. Such clubs are, generally, patronised by the élite of the school's senior school, and why not? They have a right to intellectual and spiritual enrichment at their school. We may be greatly relying on them to preserve the national culture some years from now.

There are, then, a great variety of activities available in most schools. Those who take part in these generally find them to be very satisfying elements of their school experience. 'It is great,' they say, or 'It is magic' or 'I love it'. In after-years, they often recall, with nostalgia, these activities. They are more memorable than the curricular subjects. The experience of school activities must be of significance. In what way? In answering this question we must try to avoid arguing that they are a preparation for life. They may be. But there is no means of knowing.

Broadly speaking, participation in clubs or sports or school entertainments brings teachers and pupils into a new relationship. Whereas in the classroom they seem to be pulling in different directions, in the activity they are on the same side. The pupils are in grim contention against another school out there on the pitch; the teacher is on the touchline willing them to win. Teacher and pupil are in the same brotherhood. The teacher is relaxed; the pupil sees him, for once, as a human being, not a figure of awe. The so-called generation gap narrows. (It was always something of a fiction anyway, propagated mainly to exploit adolescents in the interests of the teenage market.) The new relationship between teacher and taught spills over into the classroom, probably with significant effect. Where friendship of the type engendered in the sphere of activities exists, the conception of discipline becomes irrelevant. And out in the school community, the more pupils take part in the activities and the more teachers are prepared to organise them, the stronger will be the bonds that bind them all together in cordiality.

Another obvious effect of these corporate activities is that they narrow the gap between the academically successful and the academically inadequate, between the two societies the existence of which is the problem overriding all others in the comprehensive school. In the activities, the pupil who was a dismal failure in class work gets a new deal. He may be the most skilled of all the school's footballers; she may be the obvious choice for the leading soprano part in the school cantata. So the imbalance is reduced and they come into their own. Moreover, pupils who drew away from one another because of academic differences may join forces again in the rugby team or in the preparation of the school mannequin parade. The school community draws strength from such realignment. The school authorities should encourage it. They should go further: they should contrive it.

From the pairing of academic and non-academic pupils in activities friendships will blossom, especially if the activities are of an arduous nature as, for example, cross-country running, hill-climbing, survival courses, gymnastics and trampolining. To have known exhaustion or fear in the company of friends — that is one of life's most memorable experiences. The fires of danger forge unbreakable links, as old soldiers know. Similarly to exhaust yourself in some great enterprise leaves neither time nor inclination for petty conflict.

Theoretically school activities should provide individual pupils with the opportunity to try themselves out in activities which are new to them. Education is sometimes thought of as a voyage of discovery into oneself; several talents or interests may repose, like many other mysterious entities, in one's subliminal self, awaiting only to be stimulated or called into active being. Abilities in music, acting or sport may well come to light if the pupil can only be induced to make trial of a new activity. From such discovery the prospect of a career may emerge; or an interest in a hobby may be aroused to be carried over into later life and bring years of contentment and pleasure. In the future years, envisaged by silicon chip scientists, the wasteland of leisure will be desolate indeed if TV, bingo and drink are to be our only solace. The schools should, at least, point the way towards leisure-time activities that will absorb, satisfy and delight.

In most activities the pupils play a part in the organisation. They may select teams, see that pitches are lined, write to the secretaries of other schools' teams for fixtures, act as hosts to visiting debating teams, canvass in the town for advertisements for the school magazine, post notices on the boards, manage the sale of programmes and ices at the school show, book bands for the discos, in short — perform the dull routines without which no event can take place. Most of them have, for long, been accustomed to adults discharging such preparatory duties. When young people attempt to organise, they often blunder. They do not realise the crucial importance of detail and of checking, twice and thrice, the vital links in the chain on which success depends. Arrangements for extra-curricular events should often be made their responsibility so that they may learn in the hard school of experience.

Similarly, they should have experience of decision-making. Small committees of pupils should discuss and decide policy for, say, the fair use of the table-tennis facilities, the choice of evening for the school dance, the age limit for admission to the debating society, the programme for the variety musical show to be presented by the house, or the periodicals to be made available in the library or common room. Thus they will learn the operations of democracy and the unpalatable fact that you do not always get your own way.

In most activities, pupils are not long in discovering that they are dependent on one another playing the parts allotted to them. This is, of course, probably the main tenet of the school's ethical code and there is no better medium for displaying it than in the extra-curricular field. In most activities pupils have to work together in close combination. An inefficient unit damages the whole outfit. In sports teams each player is expected to play the part appropriate to the position he occupies. In hill work a single person, who has been careless about his equipment, may become a danger to the whole group. An actress who misses the final rehearsals for the school play, forgets her words 'on the night' and spoils the show. The badminton secretary who forgets to purchase the shuttlecocks as he promised to do at the last committee meeting deprives the whole club of their evening's enjoyment. That we depend on one another is a social axiom, apart from being a cornerstone of the Christian ethic.

Related to all this is the conception of service which is a basic feature of many school activities. Where competitions with other schools are involved, as for example, debating or general knowledge contests, pupils know, without being told, that at the time of the encounter the school's reputation is, or at least seems to be, in their keeping. For the duration of the competition, they are the school. Chauvinism is an unpopular commodity nowadays, but doctrinaire egalitarians, sneer as they like, will never prevent young people from feeling proud that they performed in public under the banner of the school and wrote a fresh and not ignoble page in its history, whether it was in a football final, or a cross-country race, or an ambitious operatic production. 'Rest after toil' often brings measureless content but it is never more delectable than when it has been experienced in serving a cause larger than oneself.

People who have taken a full part in the extra-curricular life of the school will usually make a clear distinction between the transactions of the classroom and the corporate activities outside. The distinction is real, else why should they remember the latter so much more vividly than the former? One obvious difference is, of course, that the work of the classroom is obligatory while the other is voluntary. Moreover, since few would volunteer for activities unless they were capable of the exercises involved, the activities may spell achievement while the classroom may be associated with failure. Again, much of the classroom activity is of a routine nature, its operations predictable and, therefore, unreal, artificial. It presents contrived situations, simulacra of real life. Such exercises will offer their own brand of fascination to pupils inclined to manipulate them and intelligent enough to visualise the reality they prefigure but the majority, ill equipped for this kind of perception will soon, like the Lady of Shalott, grow 'half-sick of shadows' and find more gratification in the reality of the extra-curricular activities.

Participation in several activities, provided these are competently organised, will extend the pupil's experience significantly. These new experiences may be physical, like judo, diving, surfing, skiing or trampolining; intellectual, like taking part in a physics project or constructing a computer; emotional, like performing in a Shakespearean tragedy, singing in a principal part in an opera or finishing the course in a ten-mile cross-country event. Naturally projects, activities, sports and theatrical shows will vary as to the intensity of the emotion engendered. But they are all real in a sense that classroom lessons are not. And some of them anyway may reveal to the participant certain truths about life: that it is infinite in its variety, bewildering in its complexity and limitless in its capacity to surprise.

Several features of the school experience to be found in school activities are worthy of special consideration. These are: preparatory activity, working at something with an end in view, a display, an exhibition of work or a theatrical show; resourcefulness, meeting unpredictable situations and finding resources within oneself to cope with them; discipline, acceptance of the fact that in certain activities success is impossible unless one obeys the rules or the directions of a leader implicitly; the discovery of confidence in oneself when, as a result of training and leadership, one has done something he has thought to be beyond one's powers and has no doubt about one's ability to repeat the achievement; spiritual elevation, i.e. perception, perhaps only momentary, of new levels of reality in music or language or in nature.

These elements will be most frequently discernible in sport, in adventure courses, in school stage shows, in drama, music and dance. Let us look at these activities a little more closely.

First, sport and athletics. Sports have this in common, that the maximum pleasure is experienced only when one plays well and playing well involves training and coaching, in short, discipline. The special delight of games is reaching the stage where one's body will obey one's mind, instantly and wholly, to perform intricate, smooth, nimble movements to meet the particular situations that confront the player during the game. Self-control is paramount. And it is paramount, too, in the code of games ethics that ought to be established by everyone who organises sports in schools. Many practices, normal at professional football games, have crept into school football: so-called professional fouls; questioning of the referee's decisions; time-wasting when one's team is winning; arrogant posturing of players when they have scored goals; insolent and obscene chanting by spectators; and offensive gloating over opponents when one's team is in the lead.

If football is to be retained as a school sport (and in view of behavioural deterioration of spectators and the lack of sportsmanship in so many players, this is questionable), all those who organise the game at school will have to present alternative modes of conduct to the children. Discipline, again, is the key. Children must learn to be modest in victory, dignified and sportsmanlike in defeat. I recall a Scottish Shield final at Hampden. Victors and losers were lined up for the ceremony of presenting the trophy, some of the losers in tears. But the losing captain crossed to his opponents and went down the line shaking everyone by the hand. I thought of Marvell's lines about Charles the First:

'He nothing common did or mean
Upon that memorable scene.'

That is how it should be. Teachers will find it hard to counteract the vicious trends in modern sport but they must try. Otherwise we will breed a generation to whom sportsmanship is an unintelligible idea. Once again the required change in attitudes will largely depend on the teacher's example. He must refrain from criticising referees, condoning gamesmanship, recommending illegal tactics. The conception of dignity in sport should underlie his training of teams. His players should not display childish petulance or ill temper. Their demeanour should be appropriate to the school's ideal of good citizenship and self-respect.

In a healthy community games players will be actuated by their loyalty and will give all they have of skill and effort to win the matches for the school. But organisers must beware. To concentrate too intensely on the winning of trophies in inter-school competitions might not be in the best interests of their own school. The emphasis should be on the maximum involvement of those willing to play, to let as many as possible feel that they are held in some regard. A house league involving fifty players is preferable to having one team of picked players representing the school every week.

That games helped to develop character was long a postulate in the public school creed and Waterloo was said to have been won on the playing fields of Eton. Has this agreeable notion any validity? Perhaps it is more likely that persons with strong characters are attracted to games than that games strengthen character. None the less, on the sportsfield situations arise where courage and fortitude and resolution are demanded of a player by the nature of the situation in which he finds himself. Now all human beings possess these qualities in varying degrees. Some do not realise that they have them until they find themselves in the testing situation. And, in some cases, people put themselves into the testing situation to discover whether they have them or not, as we are told many mountaineers do. Those who possess them in meagre quantities may be raised to high levels of heroic performance if there is at hand the right kind of teacher, who will transmit to the feeble one some of his own virtue. It is, therefore, important to have that kind of teacher in charge of games, a leader, well respected, capable of demonstrating to the pupils, with confidence, how one copes with the unnerving situation.

I know a young gymnastics teacher who welcomes into his trampolining team any who care to apply. After some months they are all able to take part in a display as awesome as it is spectacular. The pupils advance in three columns, coming from three different directions, to leap on to a trampoline and over a horse, the operation being so timed that each performer makes his leap a split-second before one from the second column, with a pupil from the third column following closely behind. The success of the exercise depends on the certainty that no one's nerve will fail at the moment of take-off. If he hesitates for a fraction of a second, the display will be ruined and there may be an accident. But nobody fails the supreme test because they see, at the crucial moment, their instructor standing quite still beside the apparatus and the very presence of that familiar figure transmits confidence and courage. This is a paradigm of how pupil and teacher should relate to one another in the school experience.

In team games the encouragement may come from the captain of the team if he or she has the gift of leadership. A nagging, hectoring captain will not do. The lesson to be learned here, by all concerned, is that calmness in a crisis, disciplined adherence to prearranged tactic and unrelenting effort will do all that can be done to save the day when the tide is running against the team. On these occasions the discerning participant will learn that action counts more than words and that to lose one's composure is to lose the battle.

Long-distance running will demand other virtues and offer other experiences. Here the runner is unlikely to be inspired by the encouraging voices of coach or spectators. When in dire need, it is only to himself that he will call for reserves of energy. The experience is a voyage of discovery as pure and simple as you will find in few other school sports. The runner discovers out there in muddy fields, deserted moors, darkling forests the strength of his sinews, the measure of his determination, the answer to a hoary philosophic dilemma about the relationship of mind and body. There is, surely, a unique kind of experience in long-distance running. What does the runner think about as he runs? Does he put his mind into suspension and make himself an automaton? Does he solace himself with fantasies of rest and sleep and drink and food? Is he spellbound by the natural beauty of the locality where he runs, 'the fields of glory' as the hymn says, bright pageantry of woodland and river and the ever-changing vistas of cloudland? Or is he in a trance-like state, glimpsing phantasms, hearing hallucinatory voices? Whatever is the nature of this solitary experience, there is that in it which is deeply satisfying to the soul for the act of winning does not seem so important as in other athletic activities. As the young poet Sorley wrote:

> 'We swing ungirded hips,
> And lightened are our eyes,
> The rain is on our lips,
> We do not run for prize.
> We know not whom we trust
> Not whitherward we fare,
> But we run because we must
> Through the great wide air.'

In competitive games it is helpful to distinguish between those that involve bodily contact with opponents and those that do not. Emotion seems to enter more into the former and, therefore, the need for self-control is all important. In the latter the experience is more mental and private concentration on the task is the required approach. These aspects will not be neglected by instructor or coach. But in every kind of athletic contest the experience will be mean and degrading if one has no respect for opponents and is not prepared to acknowledge their merits and join them in relaxed, friendly intercourse after the contest.

Most schools now organise activities that take pupils to residential courses, usually far from the city. Sometimes the school owns a country residence where parties can stay for weekends or longer, fending for themselves, making expeditions by river or into mountains, doing geographical or biological or geological fieldwork, or archaeological digs or meteorological recording. There are, too, permanent outdoor or adventure centres where, under qualified instructors, pupils may take part in physical exploits appropriate to the natural environment, such as canoeing, skiing, sailing, survival exercises and rock-climbing. Experiences at such places are most intense. Pupils return from them with magic in their eyes. They have had new visions of the wild joys of living that defy analysis. There is the novelty of looking after oneself in the company of one's friends, remote from parental interference, or the pleasure of forming new friendships with young people, interesting because they come from environments different from one's own. There is the scenery, strange to a towndweller and almost dreamlike to the eyes of those with imaginative propensities, the deep woods, the angry rivers, the silent snow slopes and, at night, 'the solemn constellations' pageantry', unsullied by the myriad neon lights of the city sky. And, above all, there is adventure. What is adventure? It is encountering the unpredicted and finding resources within yourself to cope with it. It is unsystematic experience which, after all, is the essence of the human situation.

Living for a week in these remote centres, normal life, at home and in the classroom, begins to appear unreal. Home life, nowadays, is dominated by the presentation of experience in an entirely illusory form by the TV screen. Classroom life is often a sequence of routines where experience is simulated to produce theoretical answers to problems, possibly waiting in the future. But in these outdoor courses nothing is in the future, nor is the thing before you an image on a screen: it is here, there is no escaping from it and it is real. And it may be dangerous. There may be a confrontation with fear. But there will be guides to sustain you and you will return to base, to food and firelight, feeling that you have travelled far in spirit as well as in body and that things will never be quite the same again.

Every school should have a rural retreat, where children should live for a few days, simply and, perhaps, adventurously in a natural environment, making discoveries about their own stamina and determination in challenging situations. There many would find a new type of happiness, the deep comradeship that comes from sharing an arduous physical challenge. To organise such experiences is to offer alternatives to the subcultures of urban pubs and discos. There are young men and women on every staff ready to be leaders in such projects and exploits, but they must have encouragement and financial help from those in a position to offer these. One may have doubts about the usefulness of some of the subjects in the present-day curriculum but most of us would agree about the paramount importance of environmental studies and of having attitudes and policies with respect to the multifarious issues involved, such as the preservation of scenic amenities or the protection of wildlife. School activities that will take the pupils to the country as often as possible should be a high priority.

Activities that involve a period of preparation for a future event, open to the public, are most likely to maintain interest and enthusiasm at a high level. What is done seems more real and meaningful when there is a clear end in view. Pleasurable emotions are involved; excited anticipation mixed with uncertainty as to the outcome gives the days before the event a new quality. Such events are recognised, in most schools, as highlights and bring widespread happiness. These are occasions when parents and friends throng the corridors and everyone, head, staff and pupils, is at pains to present as perfect an image as possible. There can be no harm at all in their doing so. 'Be ye therefore perfect' is a New Testament text of universal validity.

The event may be an exhibition of craft work or painting, a mannequin parade, a concert with the school choirs performing, a school orchestral concert, an opera, a school play, a fête — each school has its own traditional show. Each makes a significant contribution to the school experience of everyone who takes part, but much of its value to the community is lost if only a limited number of the brighter pupils are concerned. School stage shows and concerts should be planned with maximum involvement of the pupils as one of the main aims. Choirs should be as large as the stage can accommodate. If a dramatic entertainment is to be presented, thought should be given to the inclusion of many walking-on parts and these should be taken, preferably, by pupils not academically gifted and by those who do not take part in other activities. The help of such pupils should be enlisted as backroom boys, stagehands, lighting assistants, programme sellers, ushers or ice-cream vendors. Once more the policy is to recognise the place of the less able pupils in the school community and let them feel that they are not forgotten.

The ideal method of achieving mass involvement is to have every class putting on a single contribution to a week's entertainment, each group presenting a play or a dance sequence or a short musical scene. Some of these contributions will, necessarily, be substandard but must not be rejected on that score. One remembers the words of Theseus in *A Midsummer Night's Dream* when Bottom's ridiculous play was being considered for a court performance:

> *'I will hear that play;*
> *For never anything can be amiss*
> *When simpleness and duty tender it.*
> *Go, bring them in: and take your places, ladies.'*

The moral strength of the school may be assessed by the extent to which all the various departments are prepared to co-operate in the preparation and the presentation of the school show. The Technical Department will construct the scenery; the Art will paint it and do make-up; Physics will look after lighting effects; Music will, of course, make the main contribution if the performance is a concert and, if not, will attend to background and interval music; Physical Education will train the dancers; Chemistry may require to provide smoke and explosions if the production requires such effects; Home Management will make the costumes; the English Department may co-operate with Speech and Drama if the performance is a play; Business Studies will duplicate programmes, attend to royalties, act as treasurer. And all these departments will use the services of dozens of pupils in these tasks and duties until most of the school have been involved one way or another.

Experienced headmasters who have long sought meetings with individual parents, without success, will know that the only way to bring such reluctant customers to the school is to put their child on the stage in a show. Perhaps a school concert is not the most suitable occasion for informing the parent that her daughter is an incorrigible latecomer but it may be the only chance to convey that useful information.

Apart from the valuable experience of working in a team where everyone depends on everyone else for overall success, what would one hope that a pupil learns by being concerned in a school stage show?

It should be abundantly clear that final success is in proportion to the amount of rehearsal that has preceded the performance. The lesson is that there is no royal road to success; practice makes perfect.

Discipline is once more essential to the operation. Pupils who have performed in the school orchestra or sung in the choir know that the patterns of sound demanded of them by the conductor admit of no personal modification. Without his inflexible direction there will be no final splendour.

From the point of view of the individual performer, a valuable part of the experience is what we might call 'rising to the occasion'. Responsibility lies like a heavy load upon him or her — to enter at the precise moment according to the direction received, to keep self-control in spite of nervousness, to do better than he or she has ever done at rehearsals. This is experience of duty, not to be avoided, confronting one in a sharp, relentless form. Perhaps the pupil is encountering this inexorable taskmaster for the first time in life. It will not, however, be the last.

On the stage, the performers may experience what may well be entirely new to them, an audience in telepathic liaison with the performers, transmitting waves of good will towards the stage so that all seem to be sharers in a great communal occasion, 'the time and the place and the loved ones all together'. Theatrical people are acquainted with this phenomenon and count it their dearest reward.

The fact is that stage performances offer a variety of quite unique experiences, inexplicable, mysterious, occasionally terrifying. Sometimes the world presented on the stage, and normally considered illusory, by some potent magic becomes real to the performer. The actor becomes the person whose character he is portraying. Be that as it may, on the stage one's emotions are intensified — one may experience a kind of mystical joy.

For it can be a world of grace and beauty. Think of the dancers, their audience spellbound by their unearthly loveliness, they themselves for a few brief minutes denizens of a timeless world. If they could only continue for ever in this dream country of, seemingly, bodiless ecstasy, that would be the end of all desire.

Such are the stage experiences that transport to new modes of being. Personalities are momentarily merged in something vaster than themselves, something spiritual. The dancers have become the dance, the musicians the music.

Chapter 13

The School Assemblies

If the most significant fact about a school is that it is a community, then morning assembly is the most important period of the day. When all the pupils of the school, or even a largish section of them are together in the school hall, then those present are a community and should feel themselves as such. They are not, for the duration of the assembly, individuals — they are the school. Later, in their classrooms, they will be individuals, but not now.

Morning assemblies are composed, normally, of an act of worship, announcements, ceremonies and, sometimes, comments by the one taking the assembly on recent school happenings with a distribution of praise or blame, of encouragement or warning.

Most schools are too large to allow of assemblies of the whole population. It is usual for the school to be subdivided for these occasions, either vertically by houses or by a horizontal division, upper, middle and lower school. The latter distribution is to be preferred. A wide age differential makes a common response to what is being said from the rostrum unlikely.

Ideally each group should have two assemblies per week but there is one day too few to allow of this. The problem may be solved by working on the basis of a six-day week. This device may complicate the timetable and it may be necessary to arrange that the seniors have two assemblies, middle and lower school to have one each and the remaining day to be given to lower and middle school alternately.

The importance of the occasion will be emphasised by the presence of the head at every assembly. He will take the assembly, either in whole or in part. Thus he becomes part of his pupils' daily experience. He is a presence. He stands for constancy, support, perhaps inspiration. He is the continuing factor in the multitude of events that form the day-to-day history of the school, the history that is in the making. If he is the right man, trusted and respected, the pupils will expect to see him at assembly and they will find his absence disturbing.

The pupils should be seated. The atmosphere will be serious and quiet, with a slight feeling of solemnity but none of strain. The entrance of the person taking the assembly will produce silence. If he has to scream at the pupils 'Silence!' he should not be taking the assembly. No matter what promoted post a teacher holds, whether it is depute head, house master or any other, he must not be given the task of taking the assembly unless he can do it effectively. He must be audible, fluent, interesting, commanding, persuasive, with vocal technique appropriate to the varying components of the assembly.

The crucial question that must be asked about school assemblies is one that has been evaded by so many headmasters or given a faltering answer: what place should religion have in the school experience?

Some would answer that it has no place nowadays, arguing that the decline in church-going and in religious practices shows that religion is irrelevant to the world we live in. If one accepts present-day society without criticism or condemnation, then that answer is valid. To such people the fact that millions of modern children grow up without the faintest idea of the nature of religion or of its moral implications is not a matter for regret. It is just one of the facts of modern life.

It is assumed, however, throughout this book, that it is the duty of the school to present alternatives to the values and the behavioural practices of the modern world. It is recognised that ours is a sick society, intellectually shallow, emotionally insensitive, morally bankrupt, and spiritually blind. The decline of religion then is merely another instance of the sickness if not one of its causes. And just as the school must offer its pupils social and moral values alternative to those in vogue today, so it must present religion as the basis of a lifestyle more fundamental, real and rewarding than the meagre and barren ideologies of the modern world.

To take a decision to omit religion from the school experience is an action of much gravity. It is to obliterate from the body of the academic material, hitherto considered as essential, knowledge of the teachings of Jesus which have been accepted, even by those who do not follow them, as the supreme statement about human potentiality and human perfectability. It is to ignore the universality of religious practices and beliefs through the history of every race and nation. It is to disregard the centuries-long influence of religion, and particularly the Christian faith, on our history, our social life and manners, our language, our literature, our architecture, our art, our law and government, our great movements of social reform. It is to pass over the lives of the saints, the seers, the mystics, the religious reformers and all those who, down through history, have sacrificed everything, including their lives, in the service of their faith. It is to leave out of the reckoning the enormous amount of evidence accumulated in recent years, that there is reality imperceptible by our senses and beyond the comprehension of our intellects — I mean in the sphere of psychic phenomena. J. B. S. Haldane wrote, 'The world is not only stranger than we think —it may be stranger than we can think.'

There are, doubtless, many educationists who see no deficiency in a system that sends young people out into the world without any kind of faith or any conception of spiritual values. I would not care to be of their number. My belief is, rather, that life is meaningless and hopeless unless one has formed some kind of relationship, however tenuous, with the infinite. There should be a glimpse of this somewhere in the school experience.

But there are a thousand different roads to spiritual illumination, many of them overlapping and all varying in their practices and their dogma. Schools must not indoctrinate and those who organise school religious assemblies must beware of the sectarian approach of exclusive coteries and pedlars of easy salvation. Children should be introduced to religious attitudes and values, quietly, hesitantly (who can be sure?), and not subjected to and repelled by confident, dogmatic assertations of a naive evangelical nature. Such approaches are counterproductive, especially with the young — intelligent children react swiftly to those who have too obvious designs upon their minds. Religious material should be presented without theological dogma and only rarely with comment. It would be presented in the same way as one would present a piece of classical music, or a masterpiece of art. If there is truth and meaning there, it needs no embellishment. It will speak for itself by its beauty and its truth as judged by our other experiences, and by its otherness, its absoluteness, its timelessness.

It will be sufficient if the school has, in some way, offered a counterweight to the ideological materialism of the times, the widespread assumption that economic and biological factors alone have validity in the human situation.

The religious part of the assembly should be carefully prepared. It should consist of a reading from scripture or other literature and a prayer. The scripture reading should be entirely intelligible, even if some comment from the reader may be necessary. The practice of having pupil office-bearers, house captains, prefects, etc., reading the lesson is to be deplored. No one should read at assembly unless he has a clear, audible voice and can convey the mood of the passage by his expression. Such people, pupils or teachers, may be hard to find but the truth is that seldom does anyone bother to look for them. The reading of the passage is not a ceremonial act in which people holding certain positions are entitled to play a part. The passage is to be entirely meaningful to those who are listening and, therefore, only the best readers should be entrusted with the task.

In selecting themes for the assembly, one should avoid theological material that might lay one open to the charge of sectarian indoctrination. Passages chosen from the Bible or from other literature should illustrate Christian morality, either by precept as in the Sermon on the Mount or by the parables or by stories from other sources, as 'for example the tale of St Martin sharing his cloak with a beggar. As the term goes on, the pupils should come to see more and more facets of the beauty of the Christian life, of unselfishness, of repentance, of forgiveness, of compassion, of courage, of faith, of patience and of love — love, the greatest of these, love which, according to Dante, 'moves the sun in heaven and the other stars'.

The assembly is not an occasion for sermonising. The approach should be aesthetic rather than authoritarian. Virtue should be presented to the minds of the pupils imaginatively, through poetry or beautiful, memorable stories; or, if there is a competent dramatic group in the school, cogently, by the impact of a carefully selected fragment of drama with a pointed moral implication.

Passages read at assembly should sometimes relate to the kind of conduct, good or bad, which is identifiable in the day-to-day life of the school. The most effective Bible reading known to me was the shortest. There had been an outbreak of pilfering in the tuckshop. The Bible reading was announced: Deuteronomy 5, 19 'Thou shalt not steal'. Realisation was instant, the stillness profound.

If the reading passages are carefully chosen, they may be seen to be related to the ethics of the school. Chief of these should be the obligation to help the unfortunate, in the school and out of it. The theme of suffering and healing is basic in Christian living. The stories of the New Testament have a reality that is based on their universal applicability. The man beaten by robbers going down to Jericho may be a crippled boy in second year. The prodigal son is the unhappy delinquent suspended from the school for insubordination.

Other passages chosen for the assembly should convey some sense of wonder and awe. The range here is limitless, embracing such topics as the infinitude of space, the minute world of sub-atomic particle, the instinct that guides the wildfowl home, the mysteries of memory, the phenomena of ESP, telekinesis, precognition and hypnotic regression, with its implications of reincarnation, depth psychology and our subliminal selves, the complexities of the lifestyles of plant and insect, the magic of poetry and the great orchestral pieces with their intimations of immortality. Indeed the numinous may be experienced even in a drab school hall, through the flutes and violins of members of the school orchestra.

There should be a prayer, spoken by the one who is conducting the service. To some this may seem an obsolete exercise. But prayer is a universal practice which enables us to formulate our aspirations and direct our thoughts away from ourselves towards others whose need is greater than ours, pupils who are seriously ill or have domestic worries or who are concerned about their exams and their futures, or who feel that the school is presenting them with formidable problems with which they cannot cope. These prayers will imply that we wish to help the needy and strengthen us to act rather than to talk. Sometimes there should be a brief space of time, set aside at assembly, for meditation on an appropriate subject and for silent prayer. Quietism would seem to be an unlikely philosophy to recommend itself to the disco generation. Yet perhaps not altogether so, for some of their pop heroes have been to the East to learn the art of contemplation from mystics there. Sometimes the silent prayer should be directed to some given situation or need. Pupils should be encouraged to come privately to the person taking the service, if they would like the assembly to pray for someone who is in special need.

The importance of hymn-singing at school assemblies is overrated. In my view the subject matter of many popular hymns is one of the main reasons why young people reject religion. So-called revivalist hymns are particularly objectionable, for they seem to make the unwarrantable assumption that everyone in the congregation has had a conversion experience. The imagery featuring God on a throne with the saved ones eternally singing to Him, or of God's chosen navigating a Middle-Eastern river, the Jordan, to get to the blissful country, is presented in many of these hymns as if the writer was not sure whether the statements were to be taken literally or metaphorically. To modern children such ideas are outrageous nonsense. If there have to be hymns, let them be such as present the simple Christian virtues, or evoke a feeling of wonder and awe at the mysteries of creation. Hymns should be judged by their musical quality and their poetic content, but their theology should also be very critically monitored before they are presented to immature minds in a school assembly.

The contribution of the school's Music Department to the assembly should be in the form of introductory music from record players or rendered by members of the school orchestra. Such music should set the tone of the assembly and, if the pupils have been trained to listen to music, they may experience moments of spiritual serenity, more valid than the dogmatic affirmations of the evangelical hymnists.

The great dates of the Christian year should be marked by special services which will focus attention on the importance of meditation, ceremony and obligation. Observation of such dates and seasons sharpens awareness of the relationship between the human and the divine. Christmas, Easter, Lent, All Saints Day and November Second, the Day of the Dead, each should carry its own message about the vicissitudes of the human experience, of birth and death, of agony and exaltation and of the point where time and the timeless intersect. There is plenty of material about these profound matters in the Bible, in poetry and in the various anthologies published in recent years for special use at school assemblies. The sad thing is that so many school authorities give these matters not even a passing thought.

After the religious service come the announcements. Formal or routine announcements are normally intimated on the noticeboards or on the register teachers' bulletins: holiday dates, arrangements for exams, medical inspections, bursaries applications etc. But at morning assembly the announcements would be of a special kind: the promulgation of new school rules; references to oncoming school occasions like sports day, the swimming gala, the sale of work, the barn dance, the opera, the annual general knowledge competition, the debating contest; the annual school inspection; changes in the staff with arrangements for presentations; the plans for school journeys and educational outings, and many more.

When such matters are the subject of announcements by the head or other senior teachers to the assembly, their importance is being emphasised, they occupy the minds of pupils, and become talking points in playground conversations. The pupils realise how varied and lively is their school community, feel themselves to be sharers in a rich, satisfying lifestyle and become more disposed to play a part in the ongoing history of the school as it is revealed to them by the detailed recital of coming events.

A change in the rules, or the introduction of a new one, will be announced at the assembly. This will be stated precisely and repeated, so that there may be no possibility of misunderstanding. The announcement will always be accompanied by a clear explanation of the reasons for the change. An unpopular new rule will be more likely to be accepted if the headmaster can describe the amount of consultation that took place before the change was approved. If the prior consultation was with pupils or their representatives, so much the better.

When an announcement is made about an event the success of which depends on the support of the pupils, something more than a bare statement will be necessary. On such occasions the head must have persuasive powers at his command and the personal drive that lends the affair an element of urgency.

The ability to anticipate trouble is one of the most valuable assets that a head of school can have. Therefore there may be, at morning assembly, warnings of possible trouble at forthcoming events, based on experience of similar situations in the past. These warnings may range from the trivial to the serious. They may concern deafening shouting at the swimming gala, running on to the field at the end of a football cup-tie or drinking at the school dance.

There may be brief items of news at the assembly. Perhaps a member of staff has been absent ill, his condition causing concern. His pupils would be pleased to know that he is recovering, or that their classmate, long detained in hospital, is home. Perhaps there has been an addition to the staff and a word of welcome, in public, would be a courteous act, along with some reference to something of interest in his background. The assembly should be a forum for the communication of interesting news about the school, even if it does not immediately concern all the pupils. The pupils like this. They feel flattered to have been taken into the confidence of the headmaster. As their knowledge increases, so does their understanding of the problems of administration and their attachment grows stronger and stronger as the days go by. Let them, therefore, know as much as possible.

The assembly will offer the head the opportunity of commenting upon 'the state of the nation'. The life of the school is a swiftly flowing stream which, while broadly retaining a traditional, recognisable shape, is subject to the influence of currents and eddies and even new tributaries. Every other day something happens that may affect the habits of the pupils and have short or long-term consequences. Frequently an act of delinquency, if unchecked, may become standard practice. On the other hand, some innovation, at first an object of suspicion may, in the event, prove advantageous. The head observes both kinds of happening closely and, at the assembly, says what he thinks of them. This is real, close-up management, not remote control from the ivory tower.

He will mention and condemn serious delinquencies, often using the school's code of behaviour as his frame of reference. The pupils should feel that, when some misconduct is mentioned at assembly, it is serious and reflects on the good name of the school, that is to say, on the good name of all of them. But he will also praise honourable conduct that he has observed or has been brought to his notice. (His staff should co-operate in reporting such happenings.) He may sometimes read a letter praising an act of courtesy or helpfulness by one of his pupils outside the school or one complaining of their misconduct on local buses. He may have some suggestions to make about where transistor sets may be used on the school premises, or more gentle ways of congratulating girls on their birthdays than drenching them with perfume. He may have a word of praise for the third year girls at their mannequin parade, the second year dancers at the gym display, or the senior football team in the cup-tie, beaten but not disgraced. (He praises their sportsmanship and their acceptance of all the referee's decisions.) If he is competent at handling such public occasions, he will be careful of the tone of his comments. For an important part of his duties is to maintain the morale of the school. This means that he will project a cheerful attitude, never descend to the cynical, address his audience as responsible human beings, seriously, without sarcasm or cheap gibes. Underlying all he says will be moral principles, the basis of the school's code. The standards he observes in his comments will, therefore, be consistent from day to day, from week to week, from month to month, from year to year. That these principles will be accepted and acted upon by at least some of his pupils is not to be doubted.

This part of morning assembly illustrates a more fruitful approach to social and moral education than classroom lessons and discussions about purely hypothetical situations. A school should not be a machine working in a predictable fashion by a sequence of routines. It should be more flexibly structured so that events should be allowed to happen, events that may be created by the initiatives of pupils and in connection with which pupils may take decisions and take action. Such actions may sometimes constitute suitable material for private or public comment, praise or blame. The principles that might be involved would thus be presented in a context of reality.

The matter of the assembly must be delicately balanced. Schools have moods occasioned by many various factors, weather, the day of the week, exams, disciplinary measures, the closeness of holidays, sporting successes or failures, bad press publicity, fêtes and stage shows. In assembly bad news must be countered by good, unpalatable disciplinary actions balanced by the announcement of some privilege, justice seasoned with mercy, rigid obligations softened by humour, depression lightened by hope for a better tomorrow. Thus the school will maintain a temperate climate which, as the geographers tell us, provides the most favourable environment for achievement.

The fourth function of the school assembly is ceremonial. The occasions I refer to are when something of special import is recognised by formal action which is standardised, traditional and symbolic. People make use of ritual and ceremony when their emotions are so deeply stirred that they are at a loss as to how to express them. They turn to conventional formalities, both as a means of expressing their emotions and of keeping them under control. Ceremony is quite different from ordinary behaviour and is instantly recognised as being so. Therefore it compels attention. It operates with practised ease, it may have a theatrical pattern and, if properly performed, its image is indelibly stamped on the mind. It is practised universally. If, in our schools, we are attempting to produce complete persons, we shall find a place for ceremony.

Ceremonies exist to express some shared emotion about an occasion or a situation that lies beyond our verbal range. They symbolise profound feelings and come to our rescue when we wish to convey that we are in the presence of something bigger than ourselves. Traditional ceremonies, to those that think deeply about such matters, offer links with the past, with our predecessors who stood in that place and shared the same experience. They bring to mind the continuing history of the school.

A school ceremony will be appropriate when the school is stirred by some powerful emotion, pride in an illustrious achievement, such as conspicuous academic success or the winning of a national trophy; or, perhaps, gratitude for having had the friendship of some well-loved teacher now departing and sorrow at his going; or the inconsolable sadness of the last minute of one's schooldays, perhaps the pupil's first encounter with finality.

The appropriate recognition of these moments will be ceremonial. There are schools where leavers file out by a door opened only on that occasion, accompanied by grave, quiet music. Elsewhere a rose is placed on the lectern for each teacher in a small staff. When a cup has been won, the whole team files on to the rostrum and the head greets them individually by handshake.

The clinical educationists, the grey men, who have discarded such proceedings as childish charades, know little of human nature. Take all the colour, the pomp, the glory, the emotional experiences out of the life of the school and the children will find these things elsewhere — among the mindless football mobs and the sectarian parades.

In some schools one of the great ceremonial occasions is the installation of the school captains, elected by their contemporaries by secret ballot, chosen because they personify the spirit of service which comes first in the school's ethical code. They appear on the rostrum, are decorated with the traditional regalia, receive the handshake of the headmaster and speak to the school, haltingly but from the heart. There is a kind of purity in this occasion for no one could ever win that honour by any means other than recognition of moral worth. All the money in the world could not purchase the captaincy of the school. It is only for those who are 'first in the hearts of their fellow countrymen'. These two young people stand there, the world having grown very strange. The occasion has a quality of permanence as if it were extended in time.

Similar ceremonies, more low key, will mark the appointment of all school office-bearers. The formality of the occasion will emphasise that their positions are responsible and that they are trusted to discharge their duties faithfully. Throughout the school year, at assembly, all kinds of pupils will ascend the rostrum to receive the recognition of the school for some achievement, academic or athletic. Pupils from the humblest academic stream will come there, by reason of their indomitable spirit, as swimming champions or as victors in the cross-country race. Let such occasions never be looked upon as boring routines. To the chief participants they represent the pinnacles of the school experience.

It seems an understatement to say that these school ceremonies will long be remembered. The vividness with which they are etched on the memory creates the illusion of a school that has evaded the laws of mutability. There is an area in the mind where the past is as real as the present and these school ceremonies have a place in that timeless region. Decades ahead, they will come instantly to the memory when, among old school friends, the talk turns to their schooldays and the events and the people of that time. It would be unreasonable to claim that they had any educational value. Schools can turn out first-class scholars without having any ceremonies at all. It is sufficient to say that the most important of these ceremonial occasions convey the feeling, at the time they happen, that one is going to remember them and that, in retrospect, they have a visionary quality. That must mean something, though we shall never know what. But one is glad to have been there — and grateful too.

The School as 'Alma Mater'

When we use the word 'school', we have one of several meanings in mind. We may be thinking of the building; or of the process of education in general; or, as frequently in this book, the whole community of pupils and teachers, inhabiting a building at a given moment, for the purpose of being educated. But the word is very frequently used in a less definite way which I shall try to define. Let us say that a school is a continuing process, involving continually changing personnel, but possessing non-material features of such apparent permanence (as, for example, its own special organisational system, the prevailing habits of pupils and staff, its codes of conduct, its traditional ceremonies and activities) that those acquainted with that process have come to think of the whole integrated complex of its characteristics as having a living existence and a unique identity with which (I almost said 'with whom') one can have an almost personal relationship, the kind of relationship which is implied when one speaks of one's university as one's 'Alma Mater'.

How useful is it to think of a school in these terms?

The kind of relationship I have described is quite common. It is the way in which people who are members of some long-standing, admired and well-loved institution have come to think of it. One can think in that way about one's church, one's regiment or one's family, or a football club or a favourite newspaper, indeed, of anything which can be regarded as an abstract entity.

Let us look for a moment at the nature of the relationship that might exist between a pupil and his school, considered in the abstract in the way I have described above.

A thoughtful and imaginative pupil might see the school not just as an impressive piece of architecture but as a being of overwhelming magnitude. He might be deeply impressed by what he has been told about its antiquity. In the school hall he would read, with wonder, the names on rolls of honour, depicting the life of the school as an infinite procession of boys and girls stretching back through the uncounted years. That he had now joined the rear of that procession would evoke feelings of awe and, perhaps, pride that there should now be links between those who had gone before and himself. He might, in a flash of intuition, see the school as a continuing presence, a communion of all, past and present, who had been admitted to its membership. He might feel, for the first time, the glow of comradeship which he would experience again and again in later years. The notion of 'the old school tie' is, of course, a threadbare object of ridicule. But social satire, however amusing, can do no harm to what is a real experience, the affinity one has with all those who have shared membership of a corporate body recognised as being infinitely greater than themselves.

The apparent permanence of this visionary eidolon will also be a feature of the traditions of which it is mainly composed. These traditions form a major part of the school experience. They give a pattern to the school year and determine the shape in which the pupils think about the school.

Two kinds of traditions may, appropriately, be distinguished, the symbolic and the functional. The former will include ceremonies such as I have described; the installation of office-bearers, the honouring of school heroes or the ritualistic departure of school-leavers. Such ceremonies are formalised ways of reacting to recurring emotional situations in the life of the school. Patterned and perfected over the years, they engrave the significant moment, indelibly, on the memory. But their value and their effectiveness will survive no longer than the experiences they symbolise retain their significance and their emotional content.

Other traditions are functional in the sense that they regularise valuable activities and special occasions in the school year. The pattern of school life follows an established sequence and the varied events, like class exams, the school parties, the swimming gala, the gym display, the opera, the Christmas service, the school sports and the prizegiving ceremony fall into their appointed places in the calendar, duly take place as planned and create the pleasing illusion of an ordered and rhythmical world. The shape of the school session is a pattern, familiar to all, and it imposes a sharp definition on the school's identity. The permanence of these traditions implies durability and strength.

Certain of these traditions intensify the school experience for the following reasons. The traditional sequence in which the events take place obviates the need for continual replanning and the participants are thus free to concentrate on quality. They will benefit from the knowledge of the performances of the previous year and they will be familiar with the standard by which they must judge their own achievements. The school will become expert in its own chosen metier and will present it to the world outside with growing confidence, as if it said, 'This is what we specialise in. We have done it for years. We think we know how to do it.' As for the pupils, their interest in the school will be heightened by the predictability of the great events in the school year and anticipation will inject an element of excitement into the communal mood. As familiarity with these traditional events increases from year to year, so does the sense that the school, which provides so regularly for the happiness of its pupils, is their second home.

Schools which are inclined to emphasise tradition usually set great store by their history. They carefully preserve photographs, magazines and programmes and the keeping of the school log, now, alas! no longer mandatory, is the faithfully discharged duty of the headmaster. A school without a history is a school without a soul. Pupils are not kept in ignorance of famous achievements of former days, or of current news of former pupils' distinctions. They are aware that they themselves are part of the continuing story and may themselves step into the school's history. The obligation to maintain the traditional standards and to emulate the achievements of the school's legendary heroes is almost part of the school ethos. The recurring theme is that each generation of pupils should try to leave the school better than they found it. The principle of service before self, service offered to the school society, is readily accepted by most of the senior pupils if, as they moved up through the school, they have been groomed for the responsibilities of their Sixth Year. The acceptance of such obligations is but a mark of their gratitude for 'sunshine in the garden'. Our progressive educationists may dismiss such inclinations as belonging to the outmoded ethos of Rugby in the times of Tom Brown, but they cannot destroy them. These feelings are natural, real and valid. To believe that a community which has conferred benefits on you deserves your service in return is a basic principle of social behaviour.

It would be profitless to attempt to analyse the all but mystical relationship that links a boy or girl with an abstraction, nebulous, illusory if you like, but of compulsive potency. It is sufficient to say that an obscure element in the human mind induces certain people to identify themselves with a non-material entity, in this case, a school. When this happens the object of their veneration becomes a main source of inspiration, offering spiritual amplitude and shedding, in a mysterious way, a splendour on its humblest acolytes.

Index